"This book is a gift. I didn't realize how much I didn't know how to pray for my children until I held it in my hands! With wisdom and love, James Banks equips parents to *love our children* through prayer."

—Margot Starbuck, author of *The Solid Place*

"Nothing moves the heart of a parent more than the need of a child. Nothing moves the heart of God more than the cry of His children. Nothing ignites powerful prayer more than the truths of God's Word. That's why I love this book. My friend James Banks is a father who has prayed in earnest for his children and found his heavenly Father's heart in the pages of the Word of God. Join him in this ninety-day journey of prayer that will be instructive, authentic, and truly inspiring."

—Daniel Henderson, president of Strategic Renewal and author of *Transforming Prayer*

"In *Prayers for Your Children*, James Banks lays out a simple plan for how to combine combustible elements—the power of God's Word, your faith in the Father, and your love for your children—so that prayer emerges as an explosive force that nothing can avert. Prayer can release the power of God into the cracks and crevices of a heart when nothing else can penetrate. Prayer can search out and disarm life's land mines before they detonate. Nothing is beyond prayer's powerful reach. This book will give you a practical plan for how you can discover fresh power in prayer for the lives of your children."

—Jennifer Kennedy Dean, former executive director of The Praying Life Foundation and author of *Live a Praying Life*

"James Banks writes from the heart of a father who knows what it's like to pray for a prodigal to return home. From praying for your children to discover the power of prayer, to

asking the Lord to give them faith that surpasses your own, James uses the power of Scripture to help you pray toward their eternal destinies. By using this book as a guide, you will not run out of kingdom prayers for your children."
—Carol Madison, editor of *Prayer Connect* magazine

"James Banks has written a book that not only helps parents put the power of prayer into action but will be a great scriptural guide to strengthen their devotional life."
—Chrissy Cymbala Toledo, author of *Girl in the Song*

"Thirty-eight years ago, the Holy Spirit pressed me to pray every day for our four children. It wasn't easy. There were times, sadly, that I failed. My prayers would have been wider, deeper, and richer had I had this wonderful resource by Dr. James Banks. I thank God for *Prayers for Your Children*. It will enhance and enrich my prayers as I now pray for twelve grandchildren."
—Dr. Alvin VanderGriend, prayer evangelism associate for Harvest Prayer Ministries and author of eight books on prayer

"For every concern on behalf of your children, James Banks has beautifully crafted a sincere, tender lifetime resource to help you 'approach God's throne of grace with confidence' (Hebrews 4:16)."
—Sarah Bush, blogger and author

PRAYERS
FOR
YOUR
CHILDREN

90 DAYS

OF PRAYING

SCRIPTURE

OVER KIDS

OF ANY AGE

JAMES BANKS

Our Daily Bread
Publishing.

ISBN: 978-1-64070-372-8

Library of Congress Cataloging-in-Publication Data Available

Printed in China
25 26 27 28 29 30 31 32 / 8 7 6 5 4 3 2 1

To Noemi Dotres.
The worth of your prayers will never
be known this side of heaven.

And he took the children in his arms . . . and blessed them.

MARK 10:16

CONTENTS

INTRODUCTION
Prayers to Love By

My dear mother, besides the pains she took with me, often commended me with many prayers and tears to God, and I doubt not but I reap the fruits of these prayers to this hour.

JOHN NEWTON

One of the best ways we can love our children is by praying for them.

God waits for us to pray so He can bring good into their lives that would not have happened any other way. He loves to answer prayer, and when we pray with even a little faith, we open the door to what only He can do. No matter what their age or accomplishments, our children always need us to pray.

The overwhelming response to my book *Prayers for Prodigals* made clear that there was a need for another book that would encourage moms and dads to pray more for *any* son or daughter with the powerful promises God has given us. Parents know they need to pray, but sometimes it's easy to stay stuck in our own thoughts, ideas, and desires for our kids. We need the fresh inspiration of God's Spirit to fill our minds and hearts and lift us to new places of grace. You might think of the prayers in this book as a launching pad for your own. The real fuel in them is God's Word, and there's no limit to where He may take you.

This book contains ninety days of prayers drawn from much-loved passages of Scripture. You'll pray for your son or daughter using the Love Chapter (1 Corinthians 13) and the Twenty-Third Psalm. You'll pray through the fruit of the Spirit (Galatians 5:22–23), every piece of the armor of God (Ephesians 6:11–18), and several other powerful passages for personal and spiritual growth. Each section begins with a brief reflection introducing the week's theme, a biblical concept helpful for living the Christian faith. The thirteen themes are Knowing, Growing, Walking, Loving, Protected, Faithful, Fruitful, Thankful, Humble, Pure, Hopeful, Overcoming, and Blessed.

All of the prayers emphasize the importance of a loving and practical relationship with God through Jesus Christ. There are an equal number of prayers for sons and daughters of any age, and you can easily adapt them by switching the pronouns ("he" or "she") as needed. Some prayers include blanks for you to fill in with your child's name. You'll also notice that when a prayer quotes the same book or chapter of the Bible frequently, the name of the biblical book is referenced only once to avoid repetition. *Prayers for Your Children* is designed so that you will keep praying after you've finished reading—that's why most of the prayers don't end with an "amen."

God blesses Christian parents with children so that we *will* pray for them. Our children are a sacred trust; they've been given to us for eternal purposes so that we might point them to our Savior. Can we ever pray too much? The full impact of our prayers for our children's salvation and every other "good and perfect gift" (James 1:17) in their lives will never be known this side of heaven. But we do know we are to "pray continually" (1 Thessalonians 5:17) as we carry out our responsibility to "bring them up in the training and instruction of the Lord" (Ephesians 6:4). We need to pray not only when there are problems in their lives; we should go to God so that their best days can be better and every day can be lifted and blessed. We have a God-given responsibility to pray for them as long as we live. And we have the comfort of knowing that because of God's kindness, our prayers can even outlive us, finding their answers years after our own lives on this earth are done.

Who can pray for your son or daughter like you can? It's not about the words you use. It's about God's faithfulness, and your heart as a mom or dad. There's incredible power in a parent's prayers—the power of "*Abba*, Father" (Mark 14:36), who allows himself to be moved by our heartfelt prayers in beautiful ways. He knows and loves our children even more than we do! Our goal when we pray is simply to bring our kids to Jesus for His help and blessing on every circumstance of their lives. They're better off in His hands than in our own.

> Now to him who is able to do immeasurably more than all we ask or imagine, according to his power that is at work within us, to him be glory in the church and in Christ Jesus throughout all generations, for ever and ever! Amen. (Ephesians 3:20–21)

WEEK 1

KNOWING

Mom's Gift

I keep asking that the God of our Lord Jesus Christ,
the glorious Father, may give you the Spirit of wisdom
and revelation, so that you may know him better.

EPHESIANS 1:17

"God has something for you to do. I just know it . . ."
Those words from my mom stuck with me. But it
would be years before I would take them to heart.

Sometimes believing moms have a way of knowing things
that are known only to God. I don't know why that is, but
I've learned it from personal experience. And it all started
with a wreck.

When Mom was pregnant with me, she had a car accident
on a winding mountain road in Southern California. She lost
control of her 1958 Pontiac Super Chief on a steep downhill
curve without guardrails. The car veered off the road and
narrowly missed rolling into the canyon below.

Al, the tow truck driver called to the scene, was a friend of the family. His service station was just down Main Street from my parents' store. "I don't know why you didn't go into that canyon," he told Mom. "The tire tracks say you shouldn't be here right now. Someone was looking out for you."

Mom never forgot that. She didn't let *me* forget it either. And the way she always put it was, "God has something for you to do . . ."

Every time something of significance happened in my life, she would remind me. Whenever I doubted what I believed or was discouraged, she'd make the point again. Like Beethoven's Fifth, she wove the same theme over and over again throughout my young life. It was *her* symphony, a magnum opus straight from her soul.

Each time that Mom pointed me to God, she was giving me a gift. But I didn't know it then. More than once when I was a teenager, I would walk into the room in the middle of the day and find her sitting in a chair with her eyes closed . . .

"Wake up, Mom."

She opened one eye and raised an eyebrow.

"I *am* awake. I'm praying. Praying for *you*."

Mom's heartfelt desire was for each of her children to get close enough to God so they could discover what she already knew. He could fill our lives with meaning and purpose that could be found nowhere else. Looking back, I'm convinced that her prayers kept me out of the bottom of more than one canyon.

A parent's prayers can summon angels. But God can use them for even more. It was Augustine who prayed in his *Confessions*, "You made us for yourself, and our hearts are restless until they rest in you." The prayers in the pages that follow are intended to point our sons and daughters to what Jesus alone can give them. What could give them more peace, joy, and fulfillment than knowing Him? Or as Jesus himself put it, "What do you benefit if you gain the whole world but lose your own soul?" (Mark 8:36[1]).

There is only one "author of life" (Acts 3:15), and only He knows how our stories were meant to be written. He alone can save us from our sins and ourselves and inspire our lives with eternal purpose. With Him, each new chapter holds fresh hope and promise, and the end on this earth is only the beginning.

> No eye has seen, no ear has heard,
>   and no mind has imagined
>   what God has prepared
>   for those who love him.
>   (1 Corinthians 2:9[1])

When we pray for our children to know Jesus, we leave them a legacy of love. What better gift could we give our children than our passionate prayers for their salvation?

BORN TO YOU!

Indeed, of Zion it will be said,
"This one and that one were born in her,
and the Most High himself will establish her."
The LORD will write in the register of the peoples:
"This one was born in Zion."

PSALM 87:5–6

I remember when I first held _____ in my arms. What a miracle!

Beautiful bright eyes and a rosebud mouth. A living, breathing gift from you.

When I recall the love I felt in that moment, it makes me wonder.

How much does it mean to you, Father, when we are "born again" (John 3:3)?

I can only try to imagine. If I multiply what I felt at my daughter's birth a thousand times over, I'm barely scratching the surface of the joy you, the "Everlasting Father" (Isaiah 9:6) and "author of life" (Acts 3:15), must feel each time a living soul comes home.

Lord Jesus, you said, "There is more joy in heaven over one lost sinner who repents" (Luke 15:7[1]).

What joy must fill your heart when we are "born of the Spirit" (John 3:6[2])! So today I pray my daughter will bring you that joy. I pray for her salvation.

By faith I can see her as you hold her in your arms and the angels gather round for a closer look:

"This one was born in Zion" (Psalm 87:6)!

What could compare "with the infinite value of knowing" (Philippians 3:8[1]) you?

Oh, for her to know the limitless life you give, because your Spirit lives within her and her body is "a temple" set apart for you (1 Corinthians 6:19[2]).

May she give herself to you because you "bought" her "with a high price" through your death on the cross (v. 20[1]).

May she drink deeply from you, "the spring of living water" (Jeremiah 2:13), and "never thirst" again (John 4:14[3]).

Jesus, may she live for you above all things and "never fall away" (2 Peter 1:10[1]) so that she "will receive a rich welcome" into your "kingdom that lasts forever" (v. 11[4]).

I praise you, Father, because you are "more powerful than anyone else," and "no one can snatch" us out of your hand (John 10:29[1]).

May her name be written in your "book of life" (Revelation 20:12)!

May she know your promise to be true in her heart: "Fear not, for I have redeemed you; I have called you by name, you are mine" (Isaiah 43:1[2]).

"How great a love" (1 John 3:1[5]) you have "lavished on us, that we should be called" your children (v. 1). I pray she will be yours forever!

DECLARING DEPENDENCE

As for me, far be it from me that I should sin against the LORD by failing to pray for you.

1 SAMUEL 12:23

Father, please help me to take Samuel's words to heart.

I don't want to sin against you by "failing to pray" for my child (1 Samuel 12:23).

You've given him to me so that I might pray for him and encourage him to know you.

If I don't pray for him, who will?

Help me to follow your example in this, Jesus.

"During the days" of your "life on earth," you "offered up prayers and petitions with fervent cries and tears" (Hebrews 5:7). Help me to learn how to pray like that.

You "would often slip away to the wilderness and pray" (Luke 5:16[5]).

You were entirely "without sin" (Hebrews 4:15[5]) yet felt the need to pray, so how can I not?

Thank you for the blessings you give when we come to you. "You faithfully answer our prayers with awesome deeds, O God our savior" (Psalm 65:5[1]). I don't want my child to miss a single one!

Jesus, help me to set an example for my child in prayer. Help me to stay close to you so that I "pray continually" (1 Thessalonians 5:17).

And if he catches me on my knees when I "go into" my room and "close the door and pray" (Matthew 6:6), may it be a declaration of dependence on you that he always remembers.

You open doors when we pray, doors beyond our imagining.

You are "the One who breaks open the way" (Micah 2:13), and what you open "no one can shut" (Isaiah 22:22).

How kind you are, Father, to give us the privilege of prayer. What incredible things can be accomplished!

I pray my son will grasp this too, and walk faithfully with you.

May he learn to pray in such a way that his heart grows bigger; I ask that he will be so caught up in the wonder of your love that he takes your interests to heart. Then, when he discovers the things that you are after, he will "know that" you hear him (1 John 5:15[2]) and will be blessed all the more.

May your "face shine upon" him (Numbers 6:25[3]) so that he sees you move in answer to prayer again and again!

Show him the goodness of all that you are, Lord, so that he "calls on your name" and "strives to lay hold of you" (Isaiah 64:7).

"There is none like you, Lord; no deeds can compare with yours" (Psalm 86:8).

"What joy for those you choose to bring near" (65:4[1]), who live out their days with you!

"YES, JESUS LOVES ME"

I want to know Christ and experience the mighty
power that raised him from the dead.

PHILIPPIANS 3:10[1]

"Jesus loves me, this I know, for the Bible tells me so."

I want _____ to always know that you love her, Jesus.

I pray she may be assured of your love, because you "dwell" in her heart "through faith" (Ephesians 3:17[2]).

You've given your life for her; I pray she'll discover the fulfilling adventure that you long to write for her.

You are the "one who is life itself" (1 John 1:2[1])!

May she have a relationship with you that keeps growing deeper as she herself grows.

May she embrace the good news about you "like treasure" (Matthew 13:44[2]), the most valuable thing in her life.

May she receive the beauty of your peace, "which exceeds anything we can understand" (Philippians 4:7[1]).

I pray she'll always take comfort in your love, because through you our "comfort abounds" (2 Corinthians 1:5), giving fresh strength.

May you be her last thought when she lays her head on a pillow at night and her first thought when she gets up in the morning.

I pray she'll "sing and make music" in her heart to you (Ephesians 5:19) as her heart is filled to overflowing with your Spirit.

May she discover your purposes for her, because apart from you we "can do nothing" (John 15:5²).

I pray she'll come to understand with all her "heart and soul that not one of all the good promises" you have given her will ever fail (Joshua 23:14).

Sometimes I think of myself as someone who gave her life—but in reality, her every breath is a gift from you.

I pray she'll discover your strength by following you even when it is difficult, turning from herself to you.

May she know you as "the God who answered my prayers" when she needs it most (Genesis 35:3¹). May she say of you, "He has been with me wherever I have gone."

And when she thinks of heaven, may she think of you most of all!

I ask that she may know your "mighty power" that gives life (Philippians 3:10¹) throughout her years, so that no matter how old she grows, she'll always "look forward" to you (2 Peter 3:12).

HEART KNOWLEDGE

When I discovered your words, I devoured them.
They are my joy and my heart's delight,
for I bear your name,
O LORD God of Heaven's Armies.

JEREMIAH 15:16[1]

I pray _____ will be a man of your Word, Father.

What better way to know you than by meeting you in your Word?

But I don't just pray for head knowledge—the "religious experts" who encountered Jesus had that, and they still didn't recognize you.

I pray for a knowing in his heart, because academic knowledge alone "puffs up while love builds up" (1 Corinthians 8:1).

I pray he will know you personally by meeting you in the Bible and falling in love with you there.

I think of moments we've had together in your Word. It was as if you were in the room with me, sitting right beside me.

Even when I didn't sense your presence, how often a verse would come back to me later, showing me you were there all along and preparing me for whatever I might face.

How you speak to us through your Word, guiding and guarding and teaching us!

I ask that you, "the God of our Lord Jesus Christ, the glorious Father," may fill him with "the Spirit of wisdom and revelation, so that" he "may know" you better (Ephesians 1:17).

I pray that every day he'll have a fresh understanding of how your Word applies to his life.

"All Scripture is God-breathed" (2 Timothy 3:16). Breathe life into him through the power of your Spirit, Lord!

May he be like a hungry man at a feast, satisfied and strengthened with every bite of your truth. May your words be his "joy" and his "heart's delight" (Jeremiah 15:16[1]).

May he "listen" to you and "eat what is good" (Isaiah 55:2[1]). Then he "will enjoy the finest food," sustenance that only comes from you.

Teach him "Your way, LORD," so he "will walk in Your truth" (Psalm 86:11[5]). Give him "an undivided heart" (v. 11) so that you are what matters most to him.

"Every word" you speak "proves true"; you are "a shield to all who come" to you for "protection" (Proverbs 30:5[1]).

"O Lord, you are a great and awesome God!" (Daniel 9:4[1]). You faithfully "keep your promises of unfailing love to those who love you and obey your commands."

I pray he will love you and love your Word so he may know your joy forever!

"I'VE GOT YOU!"

For you have delivered my soul from death,
my eyes from tears,
my feet from stumbling;
I will walk before the LORD
in the land of the living.

PSALM 116:8–9²

Skinned knees, bumps and bruises . . .

I haven't always been able to catch her in time, Father.

I know I can't always keep her from pain, no matter how much I would like to or how hard I try.

She is safer in your hands than mine. She is, after all, the work "of Your hands" (Psalm 92:4⁵), just like me. And "you have delivered my soul from death, my eyes from tears," and "my feet from stumbling" (116:8²).

Where would I be without you, Jesus?

What would have happened to me if you didn't hold me "in your hands" (31:15)?

You've helped me so many times! There is no better place to be than in your care.

I long for her to hear your Spirit whisper, "Don't be afraid, for I am with you. Don't be discouraged, for I am your God. I will strengthen you and help you. I will hold you up" (Isaiah 41:10¹).

"I've got you!" That's what I'd tell her when she would trip and fall and I was there to catch her.

That's also what I'd say when she would run and jump into my arms just for the joy of it.

Oh, for her to hear *you* say that! I pray that my daughter will take a leap of faith into your arms, and that you will lift her to new heights of your love.

I ask that she may genuinely know you and run to you every day that she lives on this earth.

"Those who know your name trust in you, for you, LORD, have never forsaken those who seek you" (Psalm 9:10).

You are "able to keep" her from "stumbling" and to present her before your "glorious presence without fault and with great joy" (Jude 1:24).

Your strong hands, "pierced for our transgressions" (Isaiah 53:5), will catch her every time.

You are "the faithful God" (Deuteronomy 7:9[1]). You lavish your "unfailing love on those who love" you and obey you.

I pray she *will* love you and follow you faithfully. All the help and comfort I could ever hope to give her would never compare with "the beauty" of your presence (Psalm 27:4) and your Spirit in her, because your "Spirit joins with our spirit to affirm" that we are your "children" (Romans 8:16[1]).

May she know without a doubt that she is yours, and live each day thanking you for it!

ASKING WELL

God said to Solomon, "Because your greatest desire is
to help your people, . . . I will certainly give you the
wisdom and knowledge you requested. But I will also
give you wealth, riches, and fame such as no other king
has had before you or will ever have in the future!"

2 CHRONICLES 1:11–12[1]

I'm reminded of how you blessed Solomon when he asked
wisely.

You blessed him beyond what he expected because his "greatest desire" was to help his people (2 Chronicles 1:11[1]). He
didn't ask for "wealth, riches, and fame" for himself. He
didn't even ask for "a long life." He just wanted what was
best for someone you cared deeply about.

I want to take that example to heart. So today I ask you to
bless my child, Lord, knowing that I will be blessed when
you do.

You have said you will show "love to a thousand generations
of those who love" you (Deuteronomy 5:10).

I do love you, Lord! And I praise you that you want to show
your love for generations to come.

I cannot presume to know all of what is best for my child. I
need you to show me, so I ask for wisdom in asking.

I have so many thoughts, dreams, and even ambitions for
him, Father. Please help me to submit all of them to you and
be your servant for my son's salvation.

I ask that you "give" me more of your "Holy Spirit" just as you promised (Luke 11:13), so that I might learn to want what you want for him.

Your plans for him are perfect. You are "the Awesome One" (Psalm 76:11[1])!

Help me always to point _____ to you, so that he might seek "your face with all" his heart (119:58).

Lord Jesus, you "called the children" to yourself (Luke 18:16). I pray he'll hear you calling and draw near. May he always want to be close to you!

May he "live by faith" in you, "the Son of God," because you love him (Galatians 2:20[2]).

May he live out his days in love with you!

You gave yourself up "for our sins, just as God our Father planned, in order to rescue us from this evil world in which we live" (1:4[1]).

Please help him to know what you have rescued him from and be grateful to you for it.

May he "live a life filled with love" (Ephesians 5:2[1]), thankful for your goodness, aware that "you are near" (Psalm 119:151).

"What joy for those who trust in you" (84:12[1]). I pray that He will! There is no greater blessing than you.

WHERE THE WILD THINGS WERE

For you were once darkness, but now you are light
in the Lord. Live as children of light (for the fruit
of the light consists in all goodness, righteousness
and truth) and find out what pleases the Lord.

EPHESIANS 5:8–10

Today I pray that _____ will know the change that only you can make in a life, Father.

How easy it is for us to tell ourselves, "I've always been this way," and to doubt we can leave old, wild habits of the heart behind.

But you change hearts every day. "Anyone who belongs to Christ has become a new person. The old life is gone; a new life has begun!" (2 Corinthians 5:17[1]).

Real change is possible with you!

Where there was once chaos, you give us new strength. "You have rescued me from death; you have kept my feet from slipping. So now I can walk in your presence, O God, in your life-giving light" (Psalm 56:13[1]).

I thank you that I don't struggle with some of the things I once did. Even though I "stumble in many ways" (James 3:2), you've changed my heart. Deep inside I no longer want the old ways. I want yours!

I pray that _____ will too. "What counts is the new creation" (Galatians 6:15). May you live through her with your life-giving power as she gives up her will and her ways to you.

I pray she'll come to the place where she can say, "It is no longer I who live, but Christ lives in me. So I live in this earthly body by trusting in the Son of God, who loved me and gave himself for me" (2:20[1]).

Keep her from the trap you warn about: "These people come near to me with their mouth and honor me with their lips, but their hearts are far from me" (Isaiah 29:13).

Let her be honest about those places where she struggles with sin so that she may discover how intimately you care for her—and how transformational your power and love are!

How good you are, Lord! You delight "in those who fear" you, "who put their hope" in your "unfailing love" (Psalm 147:11).

"Let your face shine" on her, Lord (31:16). Transform her through "your unfailing love"!

May she know the soul-satisfying happiness of your smile and say: "O LORD, I am your servant; yes, I am your servant, . . . you have freed me from my chains" (116:16[1]).

May she know the chain-breaking, "glorious liberty of the children of God" (Romans 8:21[3]), who praise you as one, saying, "Yes, the LORD has done amazing things for us! What joy!" (Psalm 126:3[1]).

GROWING

Marks in God's Doorway

But grow in the grace and knowledge of our Lord and Savior
Jesus Christ. To him be glory both now and forever! Amen.

2 PETER 3:18

We have a doorframe at home that I refuse to paint. I've
put a few coats on the room around it several times,
but never on the frame. I won't even scrub it. When I clean
around the frame, it's with all the care of an archaeologist
preserving a priceless artifact. And if we ever move from the
house, I'm taking that part of the doorframe with me.

Why? Because of several simple lines in ink, each one with
a name and date: growth marks placed there for every year
of our children's lives.

I put each line there, one by one. Some years they were
very close to each other, and then came the growth spurts.
But every mark was a milestone.

Looking at those lines makes me wonder if God does

something similar with us, marking the moments and celebrating bursts of growth . . .

You do the right thing and avoid the wrong because you know if you did otherwise it would "grieve the Holy Spirit" (Ephesians 4:30). God pulls out His pen.

You choose to forgive someone without their having to ask you. God draws a line with an exclamation point!

You sacrifice to serve because you're doing it for Jesus. God marks the moment in red and stands back and smiles. Every mark matters. Even the lowest line on the doorway fills His heart with love.

Sure, I'm just speculating, and it all sounds so sentimental. But why not? When it comes to growth, we're standing on solid scriptural ground. We are to "grow up" in our "salvation," Peter tells us, once we "have tasted that the Lord is good" (1 Peter 2:2–3). He also reminds us to "grow in the grace and knowledge of our Lord and Savior Jesus Christ" (2 Peter 3:18). Once we are "born again" (1 Peter 1:23), something would be desperately wrong if we didn't keep on growing.

It's not about legalism; it's about love. Jesus said, "If you love me, you will keep my commands" (John 14:15[2]). But no matter how much progress we make, it's always growth in grace, as Peter put it. We walk in the strength Jesus gives and not our own.

We all have growing to do. In light of eternity, even the most mature believer on this earth is still very young—still standing in God's doorway. And that's where our prayers come in.

Paul wrote to the church in Colossae, "Since the day we heard about you, we have not stopped *praying for you. We continually ask* God to fill you with the knowledge of his will through all the wisdom and understanding that the Spirit gives, *so that* you may *live a life worthy of the Lord and please him in every way*: bearing fruit in every good work, *growing* in the knowledge of God, being strengthened with all power according to his glorious might" (Colossians 1:9–11).

There's a clear connection here between faithful, consistent prayer for others and their growth in grace. Paul and Timothy were praying that the growth of the believers in the Colossian church would put a smile on God's face. That's also what the prayers in these pages are about for our daughters and sons.

God wants our children to keep growing regardless of their age. Adults look at kids with excitement and say, "How you've grown!" Is it too much of a stretch to say the great "crowd of witnesses" surrounding us (Hebrews 12:1[1]) does the same?

When we pray for our children to grow in their faith, we're praying for the very thing God longs for them to do. And He gives us this assurance in His Word: "This is the confidence we have in approaching God: that if we ask anything according to his will, he hears us" (1 John 5:14).

God is listening. Go to Him in faith and ask away.

GROWING UP IN YOU

Like newborn babies, crave pure spiritual milk, so
that by it you may grow up in your salvation, now
that you have tasted that the Lord is good.

1 PETER 2:2–3

No matter how much they grow, they're always our babies.

The miracle of life is such a breathtaking gift from your hand and your heart, Lord.

I could never forget the moment I became a parent. I praise you for the wonder and gift of a child. How blessed I am!

You've given me this dear one for a reason, and your Word makes that clear.

Throughout life we're to point them to you, to "bring them up in the training and instruction of the Lord" (Ephesians 6:4).

But growing up in a relationship with you is the most important thing of all.

All else pales in comparison: achievements, degrees, awards . . . "For what will it profit a man if he gains the whole world and forfeits his soul?" (Matthew 16:26[2]).

Father, help me to love this one you have given me through my prayers.

Because you have had mercy on me and I am "counted as righteous" in you (Romans 4:5[1]), even my prayers are "powerful and effective" (James 5:16).

Above anything else, I ask that my child "may grow up in" the salvation that you so freely give (1 Peter 2:2).

I pray he'll "believe" that you are "the Messiah, the Son of God, and that by believing" in you, he "will have life by the power of" your name (John 20:31[1]).

May he "taste and see" that you are "good," and know "the joys of those who take refuge" in you (Psalm 34:8[1]).

I want _____ to know your love most of all, because "your love is better than life" (63:3)!

May he know your Word, because he does not "live by bread alone, but by every word" that comes from your mouth (Matthew 4:4[2]).

May he receive what you have waiting for those who love you, "an inheritance that can never perish, spoil or fade . . . kept in heaven" (1 Peter 1:4).

Father, I pray he'll want you more than anything else, and that "your name and renown" will be "the desire" of his heart forever (Isaiah 26:8).

May he love you with all his "heart," "soul," "strength" and "mind" (Luke 10:27[3]).

"How great is the goodness you have stored up" for those who love you and "fear you" (Psalm 31:19[1])!

If he trusts in you, he "will lack no good thing!" (34:10[1]).

ROOTS AND WINGS

> But blessed are those who trust in the LORD
> and have made the LORD their hope and confidence.
> They are like trees planted along a riverbank,
> with roots that reach deep into the water. . . .
> Their leaves stay green,
> and they never stop producing fruit.
>
> JEREMIAH 17:7–8[1]

I've heard it said that a child needs roots and wings, Lord. Roots to understand where she comes from and wings to lift her where she needs to go.

So I'm asking for both.

Please give her roots to humbly comprehend that you are her Maker. You are "the everlasting God, the Creator of the ends of the earth" (Isaiah 40:28[2]).

Help her understand that her body is much more than just a mass of cells cobbled together by cosmic coincidence. You "made us, and we are" yours (Psalm 100:3)!

"Long ago you laid the foundation of the earth and made the heavens with your hands" (102:25[1]).

May she praise you for her life and every gift you've given her—never taking your kindness for granted.

When the world tells her to have confidence in herself, I pray she'll make *you* her "hope and confidence" instead (Jeremiah 17:7[1]). Then she'll grow strong in you, like a tree "planted along a riverbank" that keeps "producing fruit" (vv. 7–8[1]).

May _____ be "rooted and established in love" because you have made yourself at home in her heart "through faith" (Ephesians 3:17).

Then her roots will hold through every storm, because you are "good, a strong refuge when trouble comes" (Nahum 1:7[1]). You are "close to those who trust" in you.

If she's firmly grounded in you, she'll have wings as well!

You promise in your Word that "those who trust in" you "will find new strength. They will soar high on wings like eagles" (Isaiah 40:31[1]).

I want to see her soar, Lord, lifted to new heights of your hope and love!

"Your unfailing love is as high as the heavens. Your faithfulness reaches to the clouds" (Psalm 57:10[1]). "The heavens, even the highest heaven, cannot contain you" (1 Kings 8:27).

"No eye has seen, no ear has heard, and no mind has imagined" what you have "prepared for those who love" you (1 Corinthians 2:9[1]).

I pray she'll always have this hope, because it "will not lead to disappointment" (Romans 5:5[1]).

Then she'll be blessed beyond my power to ask, and discover that there's never a limit to the love you long to give!

CARRIED HOME

I have cared for you since you were born.
Yes, I carried you before you were born.
I will be your God throughout your lifetime—
until your hair is white with age.
I made you, and I will care for you.
I will carry you along and save you.

ISAIAH 46:3–4[1]

"I will carry you along and save you" (Isaiah 46:4[1]).

Yes, Father! That's what I want for _____.

You have saved me and carried me through life, and I'm grateful.

I know what David meant when he wrote, "Praise the Lord; praise God our savior! For each day he carries us in his arms. Our God is a God who saves!" (Psalm 68:19–20[1]).

I treasure those moments when I could carry my child in my arms. There have been so many times since that I wish I could do what I did then—pick her up and hold her close and keep her from harm.

But there's a limit to what I can do. My arms are only so strong—but yours are the "everlasting arms" (Deuteronomy 33:27[2]).

You "will not grow tired or weary" (Isaiah 40:28). You never stumble or fall.

When she was little and she'd fall asleep, I could scoop her up and place her safely in her bed. My heart toward her hasn't changed; I love her and wish I could always keep her safe. So I ask that you do what I cannot.

I pray you will wrap your arms around her and "surround" her "with your favor" (Psalm 5:12).

Because you made her, I ask that you "care for" her even when her "hair is white with age" (Isaiah 46:4[1]). Please watch over her on those days when I won't be there to help.

I pray that she will "draw near" to you "with a sincere heart and with the full assurance that faith brings" (Hebrews 10:22), so that she will know the "comfort and salvation" (2 Corinthians 1:6[2]) that only come from you.

May she trust in you "at all times" and "pour out" her heart to you (Psalm 62:8[1]), so that she may be refreshed with "the joy of your presence" (21:6) and caught up in the wonder of all you are.

You told your people once that, "your little daughters will be carried home" (Isaiah 60:4[1]). I want that for her as well, Lord. I ask that you carry her *all the way* home. I pray she will not only wake up in the beauty of your presence each day . . . I ask that when her work on this earth is done, your strong arms will bear her to heaven, and she will awaken anew to the bright morning of eternity with you.

"PICK ME!"

> Then I heard the Lord asking, "Whom should
> I send as a messenger to this people? Who will
> go for us?" I said, "Here I am. Send me."
>
> ISAIAH 6:8[1]

Choosing teams can be rough, Lord.

No matter our age, whether we're playing kickball or meeting in the office, no one likes being the last one picked.

You understand this better than anyone, Jesus. You, "the image of the invisible God, the firstborn over all creation" (Colossians 1:15[3]), were "despised and rejected by mankind, a man of suffering, and familiar with pain," like "one from whom people hide their faces" (Isaiah 53:3).

You more than anyone know how we size each other up and misjudge each other with just a glance!

But *you* don't do that, and I'm grateful. You told us, "Whoever comes to me I will never drive away" (John 6:37).

I praise you for your open arms, Jesus. Your love overcomes every rejection.

You wait so patiently for us. Your "patience gives people time to be saved" (2 Peter 3:15[1]).

You not only save us; you give us your Holy Spirit—your very presence with us—"as a guarantee" of the unlimited life we enjoy with you (2 Corinthians 5:5[2]). You've "poured out" your love "into our hearts through the Holy Spirit"

(Romans 5:5) and given us "gifts" to encourage and "build up" others (1 Corinthians 14:12).

You never stop giving, Lord!

I pray that _____ will use "whatever gift" he has received "to serve others" (1 Peter 4:10) in a way that blesses them and pleases you.

I ask that he will be "eager to serve" you (5:2), and that he will serve others for you "with much enthusiasm and on his own initiative" (2 Corinthians 8:17).

When you want to send someone to communicate your truth and you ask, "Who will go for us?" may he respond, "Here I am. Send me" (Isaiah 6:8[1]).

May the good news resound from his life "with power, with the Holy Spirit and deep conviction" (1 Thessalonians 1:5).

I pray he will "show genuine concern" for others' well-being (Philippians 2:20) because your love is working through him.

Thank you for the purpose you give us in life, Lord Jesus. You were "rejected by" us "but chosen by God and precious to him" (1 Peter 2:4), so that we may be chosen too!

I pray my son will embrace this truth with all of his heart, so that he "may declare the praises" of you who called him "out of darkness into" your "wonderful light" (v. 9).

"MORE!"

May God give you more and more mercy, peace, and love.

JUDE 1:2[1]

More!

It doesn't take us too long to learn that word, does it, Father?

We want so much. But so much of what we want is not good for us, and you help us sort that out.

I think of those times I asked you for something and you mercifully did not answer in the way I wanted . . . It was difficult then, but I'm grateful now!

So today I ask for the most important gift my child could ever have, and I believe it's a prayer you would love to answer . . . I simply ask for more of *you* in my child's life.

I will leave to your perfect wisdom what she needs most, but I pray for "more and more" of your "mercy, peace and love" (Jude 1:2[1]) to flow into her soul.

Lord Jesus, just as you "grew in wisdom and stature, and in favor with God" and others (Luke 2:52), I pray my daughter will grow in every way in you.

What could she possibly need more than you?

"Godliness with contentment is great gain" (1 Timothy 6:6), and I pray she will be profoundly content in you.

Paul "learned the secret of being content in any and every situation" (Philippians 4:12) because he found his strength in you.

Please give her grace to understand that you are the best thing in her life.

"Cast but a glance at riches, and they are gone"—they "sprout wings and fly off to the sky like an eagle" (Proverbs 23:5).

But under your "wings" she "will find refuge" and rest secure (Psalm 91:4).

"You are good and do only good" (119:68[1]). There is no one and nothing better than you!

May she say, "LORD, you alone are my inheritance, my cup of blessing" (16:5[1]).

May she drink deeply from you, so that the "living water" you give her "becomes a fresh, bubbling spring within," giving her "eternal life" (John 4:11, 14[1]).

"You have performed many wonders for us. Your plans for us are too numerous to list. You have no equal. If I tried to recite all your wonderful deeds, I would never come to the end of them" (Psalm 40:5[1]).

No matter what may happen in her life, may she always "keep on hoping for your help" and "praise you more and more" (71:14[1]).

"May your glorious name be praised! May it be exalted above all blessing and praise!" (Nehemiah 9:5[1]).

You "must increase," but we "must decrease" (John 3:30[5]).

I pray for more and more of you in her life!

GIVE TO LOVE, LOVE TO GIVE

Give, and it will be given to you. A good measure,
pressed down, shaken together and running
over, will be poured into your lap. For with the
measure you use, it will be measured to you.

LUKE 6:38

Jesus, why is it that the smallest children give so freely?

Little ones open their hands and give what's in them. They value giving more than the things they grasp.

But that doesn't last long. The more we grow, the more our hands close until they're balled in tiny fists and our little mouths are screaming, "Me! Me! Mine! Mine!"

Unless you give us grace, we never grow out of that. So today I pray that my child will "excel in this grace of giving" (2 Corinthians 8:7).

It gave you "great pleasure" to give yourself to us (Ephesians 1:5[1]). You are "so rich in kindness and grace" that you "purchased our freedom" with your blood "and forgave our sins" (v. 7[1]).

You've "showered" your "kindness on us" (v. 8[1]) and blessed us with your Spirit, "so we can know the wonderful things" you've "freely given us" (1 Corinthians 2:12[1]).

You even "satisfy the desires of every living thing" (Psalm 145:16).

Your Word says that you love "a person who gives cheerfully" (2 Corinthians 9:7[1]). May he love to give because he loves you. I pray that his "love will overflow more and more," and that he "will keep on growing in knowledge and understanding" of how blessed he is in you (Philippians 1:9[1]).

Lord Jesus, you promised that if he gives, he will receive. "It will be given" to him in "good measure, pressed down, shaken together and running over" (Luke 6:38).

I pray he'll love to give to those in need, because your Word teaches that "whoever is kind to the poor lends to the LORD," and you "will reward" him for what he has done (Proverbs 19:17). You even tell us that "whoever gives to the poor will lack nothing" (28:27[1])!

"Good will come to those who are generous and lend freely" (Psalm 112:5). May he give "generously" so that he "will also reap generously" (2 Corinthians 9:6).

"With the measure" he uses, "it will be measured" to him (Luke 6:38), so may his hands and heart be open and his measure great.

And may he love to give to *you* most of all! When he gives to those in need, may he see you in their faces and love serving you in them, until the day he hears you say, "Whatever you did for one of the least of these . . . you did for me" (Matthew 25:40).

BACK TO SCHOOL

Get wisdom, get understanding. . . .
Do not forsake wisdom, and she will protect you;
love her, and she will watch over you.
The beginning of wisdom is this: Get wisdom.
Though it cost all you have, get understanding.

PROVERBS 4:5–7

I pray _____ will never stop learning, Lord.

There is so much to learn, and the more we truly learn, the more we understand how much we don't know!

But you know everything. You are "a wonderful teacher" (Isaiah 28:29[1]), "whose wisdom is magnificent" (v. 29).

Wisdom comes from you. And I ask that you give it to her. You are the One who "gives wisdom to the wise and knowledge to the discerning" (Daniel 2:21).

True learning starts with you. Your Word teaches us that "the fear of the LORD is the beginning of wisdom, and the knowledge of the Holy One is understanding" (Proverbs 9:10).

So I ask that she learn to pray as David prayed, "Teach me to do your will, for you are my God. May your gracious Spirit lead me forward" (Psalm 143:10[1]).

From your "mouth come knowledge and understanding" (Proverbs 2:6). I pray that she will "listen to" your "instructions," and "store them" in her "heart" (Job 22:22[1]).

Most of all, Lord Jesus, I ask that she will "grow in the grace and knowledge" of you as her "Lord and Savior," so that she may live for you "both now and forever!" (2 Peter 3:18).

Help her to understand that there is more to learning than the mere accumulation of information. No matter how much she learns and grows, I pray she will always "crave" the "pure spiritual milk" of your truth so that she "will grow into a full experience of salvation" (1 Peter 2:2[1]).

Watch over her learning, Lord. Guide her in it and guard her heart so that she stays close to you. I pray she'll sit at your feet and learn.

"You delight in truth in the inward being," and "you teach" us "wisdom in the secret heart" (Psalm 51:6[2]).

I pray she "may gain a heart of wisdom" (90:12) by understanding that life on earth is brief and eternity is long.

I pray she will learn to value your wisdom over human wisdom. "Many are the plans in the mind of a man," but it is your "purpose" that "will stand" (Proverbs 19:21[2]).

Your "wisdom is sweet" to the "soul" (24:14[1]). If she finds it, she "will have a bright future."

So I pray that she will! "Wisdom lights up a person's face" (Ecclesiastes 8:1[1]). May hers shine with your light and love and wisdom forever.

WEEK 3

WALKING

Reach beyond Touch

> While I was yet walking in sin, often attempting
> to rise, and sinking still deeper, my dear mother, in
> vigorous hope, persisted in earnest prayer for me.
>
> AUGUSTINE

Some years back my sister and her family took a long walk. They started on the beach at their home in Ventura, California, and nine months and thirty-one hundred miles later arrived in Yorktown, Virginia. They had walked from one end of the continental United States to the other.

"Why are you doing this?" I asked my sister before she left.

"Because time passes quickly and our children are only young once. We want to slow life down to a walk."

I didn't get it at the time—I only saw the challenges and dangers. But my sister saw the chance to just *be* with her kids for a while as the world rushed by.

Once I had children of my own, I understood. There are

those moments you don't want to let go of. The soft, round cheek pressed against your own. The gentle breathing of a tiny loved one safe and warm in your hands. The little hands holding tightly to your own as she takes her first steps . . . If there were only a way to rewind life and relive those moments, you'd do it again and again.

Children grow, and gradually letting them go isn't easy. Because we love them, we wish we could always keep them from harm and help when there's a need. But as they grow, they will go to places where we cannot follow, and in time they must choose their own roads.

Still, there is a way we can be there for them. Where our hands cannot reach, our hearts and prayers can. It was Robert Browning who wrote, "Ah, but a man's reach should exceed his grasp, or what's a heaven for?"[6] Because our Father in heaven is faithful to answer prayer, through Him we can offer help far beyond any natural ability we have. And because He remembers our prayers perfectly, we can even touch our children's lives far beyond our years.

When our children first learn to walk, we hold their hands to steady them and keep them up. We cannot walk with them through life, but our prayers can steady them. You might imagine placing your child's hand in the hand of Jesus. Children must decide whether they will walk with Him in the moment, but our prayers can even help them with that decision.

This week we'll pray that our children will choose to walk with God wherever they go. These are prayers built on the promises of the Twenty-Third Psalm that point to the "good shepherd," Jesus (John 10:11). He is the One who restores our souls and brings us safely "through the valley of the shadow of death" (Psalm 23:4[2]). He meets us in our place of deepest need and leads us in "paths of righteousness" (v. 3[2]) all the way home. Without Him, we wander in hard places and are lost. With Him, green pastures and quiet waters await.

We cannot follow our children "all the days" of their lives, but "goodness and mercy" will (v. 6²) if the Shepherd leads them.

These are prayers to slow life down to a walk. The one walk that really matters.

ALL HE NEEDS

The LORD is my shepherd, I lack nothing.

PSALM 23:1

Sometimes I'm preoccupied with all that my child needs, Father. But he has no greater need than you.

David understood that you are our deepest need, and because he did, he was "a man after" your "own heart" (1 Samuel 13:14[2]).

So I pray that _____ will "long for you" (Psalm 42:1[1]).

Just as he held on to me so tightly when he was little, may his soul "cling to you" (63:8[1]). May he know your "strong right hand holds" him "securely."

When he gets up in the morning, let him "hunger and thirst for righteousness" (Matthew 5:6[2]). Only then will he really "be satisfied"!

David wrote, "When I awake, I will be satisfied with seeing" you (Psalm 17:15). So I ask you to give my son "a tender, responsive heart" (Ezekiel 11:19[1]) that seeks you and loves you.

I pray that "the eyes" of his "heart" will be filled with your light, so that he "may know the hope" you alone can give (Ephesians 1:18).

When the world pulls him away, turn his "eyes from looking at worthless things" (Psalm 119:37[3]) and let him find his heart's desire in you.

"A craving for everything we see, and pride in our achievements and possessions" are not from you (1 John 2:16[1]).

Keep him from the worries, debts, and burdens that craving the things of this world can cause. Give him wisdom to understand that "the borrower is slave to the lender" (Proverbs 22:7), and "one's life does not consist in the abundance of the things he possesses" (Luke 12:15[3]).

You have come that he might "have life and have it abundantly" (John 10:10[2]). Be his life, Jesus!

May he not need *things* to make him happy but instead learn "the secret of being content in any and every situation, whether well fed or hungry, whether living in plenty or in want" (Philippians 4:12). Let him understand that he really can face "everything through" you who give him "strength" (v. 13[1])!

"This world is fading away, along with everything that people crave. But anyone who does what pleases" you "will live forever" (1 John 2:17[1]).

Thank you that we *can* please you, Father. Because you are so "rich in mercy" (Ephesians 2:4), we "who once were far away have been brought near" because of Jesus's kindness to us through the cross (v. 13).

I pray that my son's soul "will be fully satisfied as with the richest of foods" (Psalm 63:5). May he always find all that he needs in you!

THE GOOD SHEPHERD

He makes me lie down in green pastures,
he leads me beside quiet waters.

PSALM 23:2

You really are the Good Shepherd, Jesus.

You did exactly what you said you would. You gave your own "life for the sheep" (John 10:11[3]).

Because you died on the cross to save us from our sins, if we "receive" you and have faith in you (1:12), "we have peace with God through" you (Romans 5:1). You really are "our peace" (Ephesians 2:14)!

Good Shepherd, I pray that _____ will "find rest" for her soul in you (Matthew 11:29).

You are "the God of all comfort" (2 Corinthians 1:3) who calms our restless hearts with your "perfect love" that "drives out fear" (1 John 4:18).

You even give "songs in the night" (Job 35:10)—a reason to praise you when all others fail. You are that reason! You are always "deserving of praise" (Psalm 48:1[1]).

Because you "have overcome the world," even though we face "many trials and sorrows," we may "have peace" in you (John 16:33[1]).

How my precious daughter needs you, Jesus, and needs your peace. How I need you!

Thank you that regardless of the circumstances we face, because "your name is near" (Psalm 75:1[2]), your peace is always accessible.

I pray my daughter will know your peace deeply, having the heart of those who "revere" you "as Lord," and know you as "the reason for the hope" that she has (1 Peter 3:15).

I pray she will "listen to" your voice (John 10:16[1]) and follow you through every path you have planned to lead her safely home.

May she daily "ask where the good way is," and walk with you so closely that she always finds "rest" for her soul (Jeremiah 6:16).

May your green pastures, "the richest of fare" (Isaiah 55:2), satisfy her every need.

May she know the quiet waters of your "wells of salvation" and drink deeply from them "with joy" (12:3[3]).

Wonderful Shepherd! How kind you are. Even when we have wandered, you "go after the lost sheep" until you find it (Luke 15:4).

I praise you because you have promised, "I will seek the lost, and I will bring back the strayed, and I will bind up the injured, and I will strengthen the weak" (Ezekiel 34:16[2]).

May my daughter be "your special possession" whom you lead "like a shepherd" and carry "in your arms forever" (Psalm 28:9[1])!

RESTORED

He restores my soul;
He leads me in the paths of righteousness
For His name's sake.

PSALM 23:3³

You do such beautiful things, Father!

"I am filled with awe by your amazing works" (Habakkuk 3:2¹).

I think of when my child was born. Two chubby hands, two tiny feet . . .

What a miracle you've placed in my life, Lord!

I praise you for the gift of a child. "How amazing" are the things you do (Psalm 111:2¹)! Everything you do reveals your "glory and majesty" (v. 3¹).

You even restore our souls. I think of what you've saved me from. Your Word tells me, "You were cleansed; you were made holy; you were made right with God by calling on the name of the Lord Jesus Christ and by the Spirit of our God" (1 Corinthians 6:11¹).

I praise you that because of your incredible mercy I am not what I once was.

You said, "I have seen his ways, and will heal him; I will also lead him, and restore comforts to him" (Isaiah 57:18³).

I was once "dead" in my many sins, but you made me "alive with Christ" (Ephesians 2:5). You saved me "from the empty life" I was living and ransomed me with "the precious blood of Christ, the sinless, spotless Lamb" (1 Peter 1:18–19[1]).

Once you save us, you're just getting started. You strengthen us and protect what you began, helping us grow "in every way more and more like Christ" (Ephesians 4:15[1]).

How amazing it is that you help us change so that we are able to leave old sins behind. When the devil attacks us and we "resist him," you "restore, confirm, strengthen, and establish" us (1 Peter 5:9–10[2]).

I pray that my son will also learn to rely on your power to make him new, Father. You are "the LORD who heals" (Exodus 15:26[3])!

You sent your healing power ahead of the centurion who came to you years ago, when you told him in that moment, "Let it be done just as you believed it would" (Matthew 8:13). So I ask now, believing that you will send your restoring, healing touch ahead into the moments when my son needs it most.

I believe you will restore him because you are faithful to "lead" us "along the right path" (Psalm 27:11[1]), according to your wisdom which never fails.

I believe you will restore him because it will bring "honor" to your "name" (23:3[1]).

I believe you will restore him because you have promised that you "who began the good work" in us will continue "until it is finally finished on the day when Christ Jesus returns" (Philippians 1:6[1])!

STRENGTH IN THE VALLEY

Even though I walk through the valley of the shadow of death,
I will fear no evil,
for you are with me;
your rod and your staff,
they comfort me.

PSALM 23:4[2]

You've shown us that we each have to walk our own valleys, Lord. You said that any who follow you must "take up their cross" (Matthew 16:24).

Your Word tells us that "each heart knows its own bitterness, and no one else can share its joy" (Proverbs 14:10).

There are difficult roads my child will walk and heartaches I can't spare him from—even though I long to, because I love him.

Thank you that you love him even more, and you'll help and bless him as I bring him before you.

With you, "all things are possible" (Matthew 19:26)!

So I ask that you'll always meet my child in the valley, Jesus.

You can be with him in moments and years far beyond my reach.

Even when he walks "through the valley of the shadow of death," when "you are with" him, he need "fear no evil" (Psalm 23:4[2]).

With you, "every valley shall be lifted up" (Isaiah 40:4[2])!

You can give him comfort and strength in the hardest and darkest places. You can even turn his "darkness into light" (Psalm 18:28)!

Your "light shines in the darkness, and the darkness can never extinguish it" (John 1:5[1]).

David knew this from his experience of your presence and protection. So he wrote, "The LORD is my light and my salvation—so why should I be afraid? The LORD is my fortress, protecting me . . . , so why should I tremble?" (Psalm 27:1[1]).

Day or night you "neither slumber nor sleep" (121:4). You are always watching "over all who love" and follow you (145:20).

So I pray he will. May he run to you as his fortress and live "in Your light" (36:9[3]).

Help him to choose your way when it isn't easy, and to "carefully determine what pleases" you (Ephesians 5:10[1]). May he "have nothing to do with the fruitless deeds of darkness" (v. 11).

Then, if darkness falls, he'll be ready. "Even in darkness light dawns for the upright, for those who are gracious and compassionate and righteous" (Psalm 112:4).

If he takes shelter in you, "the Most High," "no evil will conquer" him (91:9–10[1]).

May the rod of your protection and conviction keep him "from the devil's trap" (2 Timothy 2:26[1]) and the staff of your "tender mercy" guide him firmly in "the path of peace" (Luke 1:78–79), all the long road home.

A PLACE AT YOUR TABLE

You prepare a table before me
in the presence of my enemies.
You anoint my head with oil;
my cup overflows.

PSALM 23:5

When David wrote that you prepared "a table" for him "in the presence" of his enemies, it was because you blessed him even in adversity (Psalm 23:5).

I ask that for _____ as well.

I pray that no matter what obstacles she faces, she will be able to say, "I thank Christ Jesus our Lord, who has given me strength to do his work" (1 Timothy 1:12[1]).

My prayer is not that you would be on her side but that she would be on yours. Then she will always win, even when she seems to lose in the world's eyes, because your "weakness is stronger than the greatest of human strength" (1 Corinthians 1:25[1]), and your "power is made perfect in weakness" (2 Corinthians 12:9[2]).

"There is no wisdom, no insight, no plan that can succeed against" you (Proverbs 21:30).

All of history is heading in your direction. "The wicked plot against the godly; they snarl at them in defiance" (Psalm 37:12[1]). But you see the "day of judgment coming" (v. 13[1]).

It is the table on that day that matters most of all.

Lord Jesus, you promised that "people will come from east and west, and from north and south," and sit at the "table in the kingdom of God" (Luke 13:29[2]). I pray that one day I will sit beside her there in your presence!

But we have a journey to finish before we get there, unless you return today. Until the day you come back, I pray you will fill her with your Holy Spirit and anoint her with your "oil of joy" (Psalm 45:7).

Even in the middle of the world's adversity, I ask that she "feast on the abundance of your house" and "drink from your river of delights" (36:8) as she worships you and discovers the soul-satisfaction you alone can give.

May she "lift up the cup of salvation" and "praise" your name for "saving" her (116:13[1])!

I pray that she will know you to be her "strength every morning" and her "salvation in time of distress" (Isaiah 33:2).

I pray she will look for the good you can bring regardless of what the devil or the world throws at her.

May her own prayer be, "O my Strength," you are "the God who shows me unfailing love" (Psalm 59:17[1]). "O my Strength, I will watch for you" (v. 9[2]).

Help us both to "look forward to your coming" and "be always on the watch, and pray" (Luke 21:36).

"Come, Lord Jesus" (Revelation 22:20)!

RESCUED BY LOVE

Surely your goodness and unfailing love will pursue me
all the days of my life.

PSALM 23:6[1]

I'm so glad you pursued me, Lord.

You went after me to bring me home; you came "to seek and to save the lost" (Luke 19:10[2]).

No matter how much it cost you, you never gave up on me. "How priceless your faithful love is!" (Psalm 36:7[4]).

Your love hasn't just looked for me or followed me—it's found me. I can't imagine living without "your great mercy and love" (25:6).

"You are God my Savior, and my hope is in you all day long" (v. 5).

I want this for my daughter too, Lord. I pray she will always "take hold of the hope" offered to us and so be "greatly encouraged" (Hebrews 6:18).

When I think about how much I love her, I'm humbled by the truth that you loved her first. She is your creation! "You knit" her "together" (Psalm 139:13), and you "long for the work of your hands" (Job 14:15[2]).

Just as you came after me, you went for her as well. I praise you that you have pursued her with inexhaustible passion and love.

Thank you for your amazing search and rescue mission, Father. You could have snapped your fingers and called an end to everything because of the way we have all "rebelled against you" (Nehemiah 9:26[2]). Yet you did not send your "Son into the world to condemn the world, but to save the world through him" (John 3:17).

I pray she will always treasure this truth, Jesus, that you loved her so much that you died to save her!

Help her to "press on to take hold of that" for which you "took hold" of her (Philippians 3:12), so that she may "take hold of the life that is truly life" (1 Timothy 6:19).

I pray she will "have the power to understand" just "how wide, how long, how high, and how deep" your love is (Ephesians 3:18[1]).

May she truly, deeply experience your love, Lord, "though it is too great to understand fully" (v. 19[1]). Then she "will be made complete with all the fullness of life and power that comes from" you.

"Surround" her "with your tender mercies," so that she "may live" and love you now and forever (Psalm 119:77[1])!

Thank you that your "goodness and love will follow" her "all the days" of her life (23:6). Draw her ever nearer to you, and bring her home to your arms—and through your kindness, even to mine.

BARE FEET ON GOLDEN STREETS

And I will dwell in the house of the LORD forever.

PSALM 23:6

I ask that my child will be with you forever, Lord. I see him there "by faith" (Hebrews 11:13), and I long to be there with him to watch him "gaze upon" your "beauty" (Psalm 27:4[2]) and worship you "in the splendor" of your holiness (1 Chronicles 16:29).

Father, thank you for the "many rooms" in your "house" (John 14:2[2]). May he "dwell" in one of them (Psalm 23:6)!

How good it will be to be free once and for all from sin and self—the "old sinful nature" (Ephesians 4:22[1])—and run barefoot on streets of "pure gold" (Revelation 21:21[2]).

I want to do whatever I can to help him get there, Father, so I kneel before you as "your servant" (Psalm 116:16[1]).

Jesus, high above my thoughts of diplomas, career, or even grandchildren, beyond any hope or dream I have for him, your purpose matters most of all. You've blessed me with him so I may love him to you!

The single most valuable, lasting thing I could ever do as a parent is point my child to you, so that he may "know you, the only true God, and Jesus Christ, whom you have sent" (John 17:3).

I ask that you will help me to do my best to live before him as a "good example" (1 Peter 5:3[1]) so that he will be drawn to you.

Please give me grace "not to put any stumbling block or obstacle" in his way (Romans 14:13) and wisdom to show him "straight paths" (Proverbs 4:11[1]) that lead to you.

Jesus, you said, "If anyone loves me, he will keep my word, and my Father will love him, and we will come to him and make our home with him" (John 14:23[2]).

I ask that he will learn to love you and obey you so he will experience the incomparable joy of having his heart at home with you in this world and the next.

May he love to be with you, spending time with you.

I pray he will "rejoice in your word like one who discovers a great treasure" (Psalm 119:162[1])!

Beautiful Savior, give him grace to walk with you "in the light," so that he may enjoy a tender relationship with the Father because of your perfect sacrifice on the cross that "purifies us from all sin" (1 John 1:7).

May your light lead him, Lord! Then, in the city that "does not need the sun or the moon to shine on it" because "the glory of God gives it light, and the Lamb is its lamp" (Revelation 21:23), we will praise you forever and ever.

WEEK 4

LOVING

Love and an Ugly Mug

Love is patient, love is kind. It does not envy, it does
not boast, it is not proud. It does not dishonor others,
it is not self-seeking, it is not easily angered, it keeps
no record of wrongs. Love does not delight in evil but
rejoices with the truth. It always protects, always trusts,
always hopes, always perseveres. Love never fails.

1 CORINTHIANS 13:4–8

To the untrained eye it was nothing more than an ugly
mug. The paint had worn off long before, and the only
visible marking was a tiny gray hairline crack working its
way down from the rim.

But the mug stayed in use. For nearly three decades until
the day he died, my dad drank his morning coffee from it.
Day after day, year after year, that mug carried a message.
It simply said, "I love you."

I gave Dad the mug when I was twelve years old. We had

stopped for dinner at a popular chain restaurant which had several of the mugs in a display case. I overheard Dad say that he liked them, so I used the last of my allowance to buy one.

Only time would tell how much that meant to him. When you're a parent, you hang on to some things because of the worth your kids bring to them. The clay trivet from second grade decorated with smiley faces. That middle school watercolor where the paint runs together. The old worn and stained stuffed animal . . . They all have a way of sticking around just because of the love that went into them.

Love at its best shows up in the smallest and most practical ways—ways that sometimes don't make sense to a self-focused world. That's why "love is patient, love is kind. . . . It does not dishonor others, it is not self-seeking, it is not easily angered, it keeps no record of wrongs" (1 Corinthians 13:4–5). This kind of love isn't easy, but it *is* possible—because God "has given us the Holy Spirit to fill our hearts with his love" (Romans 5:5[1]).

In the next several pages we'll pray our way through all the characteristics of love described in 1 Corinthians 13, with the hope that our children's lives may be filled to overflowing with God's love. Then lasting love may spill over from them into others who see our "down-to-earth" Savior in them.

Genuine love is so much more than something we feel. It's something we *do*. These are prayers that our children may "follow the way of love" (1 Corinthians 14:1), and so follow Jesus.

LEGACY OF LOVE

And yet I will show you the most excellent
way. . . . Love is patient, love is kind.

1 CORINTHIANS 12:31; 13:4

Please help my child to understand what real love is, Father.

"Love comes from" you (1 John 4:7[1]). It was your idea.

You're the only source of true love. "This is real love—not that we loved" you but that you "loved us" and sent your Son "as a sacrifice to take away our sins" (v. 10[1]).

You are love! We can "know and rely on the love" you have for us (v. 16). Your love is entirely trustworthy, "the best way of all" (1 Corinthians 12:31[4]).

When we let you love through us, we find ourselves able to love in a way that would never be possible on our own.

Your love transforms us. The more we walk with you, the more you help us to love what you love and "keep in step with the Spirit" (Galatians 5:25).

I pray that my daughter will learn to "walk in love" with you (2 John 1:6) and will give her heart to you so sincerely that she follows you in all of the relationships of her life.

Our world is filled with so many counterfeit notions of love. We define it on our own terms and then wonder why it shatters in our hands and lies broken at our feet.

Give her wisdom to see that love is more than something we fall into!

Help her to understand that love is more than a feeling or emotion—it's something we *choose* to do.

That's why you went to the cross and "suffered for" us, leaving us "an example" in love (1 Peter 2:21), and why your Word tells us to "not love with words or speech but with actions and in truth" (1 John 3:18).

The love you give is "patient and kind" (1 Corinthians 13:4[1]); you help us to love when it's not easy and doesn't come naturally to us.

May you be the love of her life, and may you lead her in love! "We love" you because you "first loved us" (1 John 4:19[3]), and you "pour out your unfailing love on those who love you" (Psalm 36:10[1]). May she choose love by choosing you.

I ask you to help me to be so loving that she'll see your love in me. "No one has ever seen" you (1 John 4:12[1]). "But if we love each other," you live in us, and your "love is brought to full expression in us."

I want to leave the legacy of your love in my child's life, Jesus.

Your "love endures forever," and your "faithfulness continues through all generations" (Psalm 100:5)!

BRAGGING RIGHT

Love . . . does not envy or boast; it is not arrogant.

1 CORINTHIANS 13:4[2]

Let the one who boasts, boast in the Lord.

2 CORINTHIANS 10:17[2]

I pray _____'s heart will be so filled with your love that there will be no room for pride.

If he knows you and his heart is right, he'll understand that it's only through your "undeserved kindness" (Romans 11:5[1]) that he can have a relationship with you at all.

Then he'll have a story to tell! The story of how he's "received one gracious blessing after another" because your grace is not limited (John 1:16[1])—it's "free and undeserved" (Romans 11:6[1]).

Then he can humbly "boast in" (2 Corinthians 10:17[2]) your generous, uncontained love.

No one is as loving as you! May he live in love with you and always want to be where your people are, because you are always close to the humble, but you keep your "distance from the proud" (Psalm 138:6[1]).

"Oh, the joys of those who trust" in you, Lord, "who have no confidence in the proud" (40:4[1]).

May you be his "confidence"; then you "will keep" him from "being caught" in so many traps (Proverbs 3:26[2]).

Steer him clear from the false god of materialism. How easy it is for us to run after things that never give satisfaction to our souls.

Your Word makes clear that "people who long to be rich fall into temptation and are trapped by many foolish and harmful desires that plunge them into ruin and destruction" (1 Timothy 6:9[1]).

Have mercy on him, so that his heart will not "envy sinners" and he'll "always be zealous" for you (Proverbs 23:17)!

Please bless him with examples in faith that will encourage and inspire him, Jesus. May he especially "follow the example" you've set for him (1 Corinthians 11:1).

Give him grace so that he won't "be selfish" or "try to impress others" (Philippians 2:3[1]). Help him to genuinely "be humble," even "thinking of others as better" than himself.

If he does that, he'll have the "same attitude" as you (v. 5[1])!

Then he "will not be afraid on the day of judgment" and can even face you "with confidence" (1 John 4:17[1]), all because your love is at work in him.

What a day that will be!

On that day he'll join the great shout of praise with all whom you have saved from sin and death, saying, "Not to us, O LORD, not to us, but to your name goes all the glory for your unfailing love and faithfulness" (Psalm 115:1[1]).

ONE FOR THE TEAM

> Love . . . is not arrogant or rude. It does
> not insist on its own way.
>
> 1 CORINTHIANS 13:4–5[2]

He's only mentioned once in your Word, but what's said convicts me: "Diotrephes . . . loves to be first" (3 John 1:9).

I know that feeling too well. But I thank you for showing me that loving to be first really isn't love at all.

Your Word tells us to "love each other with genuine affection, and take delight in honoring each other" (Romans 12:10[1]).

I pray that my child will get this and find real pleasure in making others happy, simply out of love for you.

Your love transforms us in such unexpected ways. When we fall before you in weakness, you become "the strength" of our hearts (Psalm 73:26[2]). We belong to *you*, yet you let us call you *ours* "forever"!

You turn our focus inside out. Once we were stuck on ourselves, "gratifying the cravings of our flesh and following its desires and thoughts" (Ephesians 2:3). But when your Spirit begins to work in us, you help us understand that only "you have the words that give eternal life" (John 6:68[1]).

You turn our hearts to loving and serving you, and even give us new love for others.

You're "pleased" when we "do good" and "share with others" (Hebrews 13:16), and I pray she'll serve you this way.

Loving | 77

May she "see your face" (Psalm 17:15) reflected in others as she serves them with a heart full of faith. Yes, "make your face shine down" on her, Lord (80:3[1])!

May she also get along with others and be a team player, while still standing strong with you. Help her to be flexible and "not insist on" her "own way" (1 Corinthians 13:5[2]).

When she feels strongly about something, help her to listen, because "pride leads to conflict; those who take advice are wise" (Proverbs 13:10[1]).

When someone treats her unfairly, I pray she won't pay "back one wrong act with another" but will instead "try to do what is good" (1 Thessalonians 5:15[4]). May she have strength inside and "be joyful" (v. 16[4]), raising a "shout of praise" (Ezra 3:11) to you in her heart.

May she "never stop praying" (1 Thessalonians 5:17[4]), talking to you through the day.

Those who cannot follow cannot lead. So I ask that she'll always "follow you" (Mark 10:28), led in the strength of your Spirit and Word. Then she'll kick the world's my-way-or-the-highway attitude to the curb and humbly "walk with" you (Revelation 3:4)!

FAMILY RESEMBLANCE

Love . . . is not easily angered, it keeps no record of wrongs.

1 CORINTHIANS 13:4–5

I'm in awe of your forgiveness, Jesus.

Even when you were crucified, you called out, "Father, forgive them, for they do not know what they are doing" (Luke 23:34).

Your forgiveness is perfect. You don't make us pay for our sins; you "canceled the record of the charges against us and took it away by nailing it to the cross" (Colossians 2:14[1]).

You "never sinned," but you became "the offering for our sin, so that we could be made right with God" (2 Corinthians 5:21[1]). Your forgiveness is beautiful, Lord, the most priceless gift of all!

But you also tell us that if we receive it, we have to give it.

You said that if we "refuse to forgive others," the "Father will not forgive" our sins (Matthew 6:15[1]).

I pray my child will comprehend this, Father, and take it deeply to heart. In those moments when she finds it difficult to forgive, may she ask you to help her so that your forgiveness can flow freely through her into the lives of others.

I remember Peter's question: "Lord, how often should I forgive someone who sins against me? Seven times?" (18:21[1]).

"No, not seven times," you answered, "but seventy times seven!" (v. 22[1]). Then you reminded Peter of how we should always forgive because we've been forgiven so much.

How easily we forget this! Why do we find it so hard?

Please give her strength to forgive, Lord.

No matter what wrongs may happen to her, I pray she'll let go of the past and keep looking forward to you, "forgetting what is behind and straining toward what is ahead" (Philippians 3:13).

Your Word tells us clearly, "Do not seek revenge or bear a grudge" (Leviticus 19:18). It teaches that "wisdom yields patience," and it is to our "glory to overlook an offense" (Proverbs 19:11).

Help her to love so much that she "keeps no record of wrongs" (1 Corinthians 13:5), Lord Jesus.

You taught us, "Be merciful, even as your Father is merciful" (Luke 6:36[2]). You even said, "Love your enemies! Pray for those who persecute you! In that way, you will be acting as true children of your Father in heaven" (Matthew 5:44–45[1]).

Only you can equip her to do this, and I pray you will! Then, when the Father looks on her in love, He'll see a distinct family resemblance.

Oh, He might not say, "She has my ears" or "She has my nose."

He'll say, "She has my heart."

HIDE HERE

Love does not delight in evil but rejoices with the truth.

1 CORINTHIANS 13:6

Oh, what joy for those
whose disobedience is forgiven,
whose sin is put out of sight!

PSALM 32:1[1]

I know there will be times when _____ needs to repent, Lord.

Sin sticks out its bony finger and points us away from all that's good.

So I send this prayer ahead to help him find the way home.

You are our hearts' true home, where we were always meant to be. But sin makes us run from you, just as it caused Adam and Eve to hide themselves "among the trees of the garden" (Genesis 3:8[2]).

Today I pray that when my child has sinned, his heart will be moved to turn *from* sin and *toward* you.

May he be drawn to your goodness and understand that there can be no real joy apart from you.

I think of what David realized when he persisted in sinning: "When I refused to confess my sin, my body wasted away, and I groaned all day long" (Psalm 32:3[1]).

So many grow so old so young! Their sins weigh them down, and they "refuse to come to" you to "have life" (John 5:40).

But "oh, what joy for those whose disobedience is forgiven, whose sin is put out of sight!" (Psalm 32:1[1]).

"What joy for those whose record" you have "cleared of guilt, whose lives are lived in complete honesty" (32:2[1]) and openness before you!

I pray that your perfect love will fill my child's life so that he will "not delight in evil" (1 Corinthians 13:6).

Whenever he sins, may he be quick "to repent" (Acts 17:30[2]). Give him both the conviction and urgency David had when he wrote, "Let all the godly pray to you while there is still time" (Psalm 32:6[1]).

I pray he'll "return" to you, understanding that you are "merciful and compassionate, slow to get angry and filled with unfailing love" (Joel 2:13[1]). You are "eager to relent and not punish."

May he run to you, sick of sin and longing for something better! May the cry of his heart be, "You are my hiding place; you protect me from trouble. You surround me with songs of victory" (Psalm 32:7[1]).

Even when we bring trouble on ourselves, you still love us. When we're "overwhelmed by our sins, you forgive them all" (65:3[1]).

"Many sorrows come to the wicked, but unfailing love surrounds those who trust" in you (32:10[1]).

May your "kindness and faithfulness" be with him, Lord (2 Samuel 15:20)! May he "run to you to hide" him (Psalm 143:9[1]), so he may be safe in your love.

OUCH!

Love never gives up, never loses faith, is always
hopeful, and endures through every circumstance.

1 CORINTHIANS 13:7[1]

Sometimes things happen to my child and I think, "Ouch!
That has to hurt!"

Cuts, scrapes, splinters, shots, even words . . .

The world is hard, and we are soft by comparison.

I know some hurts are necessary. They help us learn and
make us stronger.

But I praise you for something that makes us stronger still:
your love!

Your love is stronger than all the world's hurts. "Who shall
separate us from the love of Christ? Shall trouble or hardship
or persecution or famine or nakedness or danger or sword?"
(Romans 8:35).

Nothing can, and nothing will! We are "more than conquer-
ors" through you "who loved us" (v. 37[2]).

"It is good for the heart to be strengthened by grace" (Hebrews 13:9[2]), and today I pray that my child will be strong
and brave in your love.

Hurts of the body and heart may come, but "we know that
in all things" you work "for the good of those who love"
you, "who have been called" according to your "purpose"
(Romans 8:28).

The purposes of your heart—to save and to love—stand firm "through all generations" (Psalm 33:11).

So I pray you'll help him to stay "hopeful" in your love "through every circumstance" (1 Corinthians 13:7[1]).

May he trust you, because the end of every matter is in your hands—and in the end, he'll discover that you always show yourself faithful.

You waste nothing! You're even able to take that which our adversary means for "evil" and turn it "for good" (Genesis 50:20[3]).

David saw many troubles, but he said, "I remain confident of this: I will see the goodness of the LORD in the land of the living" (Psalm 27:13). May my child join in that prayer and "live by faith" (Galatians 3:11[2]).

I pray he'll "give" his "burdens" to you, so that you "will take care" of him (Psalm 55:22[1]). You "will not permit the godly to slip and fall."

"The best-equipped army cannot save a king," but you watch "over those who fear" you, "those who rely on" your "unfailing love" (33:16, 18[1]).

When this world hurts him, may he take comfort in you and discover that you are "the Mighty Warrior who saves" (Zephaniah 3:17[4]). You "take great delight" in him and will "calm" him in your "love" (v. 17[1]). You even "sing for joy" over him (v. 17[4])!

Oh, may he hear your song and take it to heart! Then, healed of his hurts, he'll "dance with the joyful" before you (Jeremiah 31:4).

FACE-TO-FACE WITH LOVE

Love never fails. . . . And now these three remain: faith, hope and love. But the greatest of these is love.

1 CORINTHIANS 13:8, 13

When she was a baby, she'd study my face with wide-eyed wonder.

Words weren't needed. Just the look that passed between us was enough.

I wonder if heaven will be like that, Father.

We'll have new innocence, "without a spot or wrinkle or any other blemish" (Ephesians 5:27[1]), every sin washed clean through "the precious blood" of your Son (1 Peter 1:19[2]).

"Then we shall see" you clearly, even "face to face" (1 Corinthians 13:12)!

We'll look on you in love and wonder, and words won't be enough to describe all that you are.

"How great you are, Sovereign LORD! There is no one like you, and there is no God but you" (2 Samuel 7:22).

Each day we'll see something new, and we'll worship you tirelessly forever, because "strength and joy fill" the place where you are (1 Chronicles 16:27[1]). "Yours, LORD, is the greatness and the power and the glory and the majesty and the splendor" (29:11).

May the gift of your love be my child's prized possession!

Bless her with sensitivity to your presence so that she'll never want to be far from you. "Let no sin rule over" her, Lord (Psalm 119:133).

May she always "follow the way of love" (1 Corinthians 14:1) and never "turn from your path" (Isaiah 63:17[1]).

But if her "foot slips," may "your mercy" meet her and "hold" her up (Psalm 94:18[3]).

You take care of your "flock like a shepherd"; you gather "the lambs" in your "arms" and carry them "close" to your "heart" (Isaiah 40:11). May she be your lamb, Jesus!

If you carry her close to your heart, she'll know that "your face" shines on her (Psalm 80:7), no matter what. Even when she isn't able to see your face, I pray she'll trust your heart.

If she can trust that you are carrying her, she can go through anything—because your "love never fails" (1 Corinthians 13:8).

When the adversary tries to come after her, your "purpose will stand," and you "will do all" that you "please" (Isaiah 46:10).

"Sovereign LORD," you are our "strong deliverer" (Psalm 140:7). You "pour out your unfailing love on those who love you" (36:10[1]).

"Let your unfailing love surround" her, Lord, and let her hope be "in you alone" (33:22[1]).

I pray she'll have "faith" and "hope" (1 Corinthians 13:13) in you as long as she lives, and so live to love you forever!

WEEK 5

PROTECTED

Uncle Abraham, Armor, and Angels

> To Him who tucks me into bed:
> Please station angels around his head,
> and guard my child wherever he be,
> and bring him back, dear Lord, to Thee.

ROBERT J. MORGAN

A braham's nephew Lot didn't always make the best choices. When Abraham offered him any land he wanted, Lot chose "the fertile plains of the Jordan Valley" (Genesis 13:10[1]). The land was productive and beautiful, "but the people of this area were extremely wicked and constantly sinned against the LORD" (v. 13[1]). Lot no doubt knew that but still chose to move his family and settle near Sodom.

It wasn't long before he'd regret his decision. Marauders captured Lot "and carried off everything he owned" (14:12[1]). Yet even after his uncle Abraham rescued him, Lot returned to Sodom. But this time he moved into the city itself. And Lot was sitting at the city gates—a place of prominence—when God sent angels to destroy Sodom.

Even though Lot would grow to be "a righteous man" (2 Peter 2:7), like all of us he was a work in progress. You have to wonder what compromises he may have made along the way to become a prominent citizen of Sodom. When the men of the city wanted to assault Lot's angelic guests, he called the men "brothers" and offered them his daughters instead (Genesis 19:7–8[1]). Then, when the angels told him to leave because the city was about to be wiped out, Lot "still hesitated" (v. 16[1]).

But "the LORD was merciful" in spite of Lot's terrible choices: "The angels *seized* his hand and the hands of his wife and two daughters and rushed them to safety outside the city" (v. 16[1]). Why? Because someone was praying for Lot. Verse 29 makes this clear: "But God had listened to Abraham's request and kept Lot safe, removing him from the disaster that engulfed the cities on the plain."[1]

As the parent of a former prodigal, I love those verses. They show me how God intervened powerfully in the life of someone who was making bad choices, and how that intervention came in answer to prayer. He even sent His angels to grab Lot's hand and pull him out of harm's way. And it might not have happened if Abraham hadn't asked.

This week we're asking for every piece of "the full armor of God" (Ephesians 6:11) for our sons and daughters. Our children need us to pray for their protection so they may "be strong in the Lord and in his mighty power," able to take their stand "against the devil's schemes" (vv. 10–11).

These are prayers that our children will stand in the strength only God can give—today, tomorrow, and always.

SOUL ARMOR

Put on the full armor of God, so that you can take your
stand against the devil's schemes. . . . Stand firm then,
with the belt of truth buckled around your waist.

EPHESIANS 6:11, 14

"May your love and faithfulness always keep" my son "safe,"
Father (Psalm 40:11⁴).

Your Word tells us that our "adversary the devil walks about
like a roaring lion, seeking whom he may devour" (1 Peter
5:8³). So I pray _____ will "resist him, standing firm in
the faith" (v. 9).

To do that, he needs armor for his soul that only you can
give. May your truth wrap around him and hold him secure.

He needs your truth to fill his mind and heart, and "your
word is truth" (John 17:17²). You "speak the truth" and
"declare what is right" (Isaiah 45:19²).

Because "you delight in truth in the inward being" (Psalm
51:6²), I pray he will love your Word and take it to heart.

Let your Word enter his mind as he goes through the day. May
"the word of Christ dwell" in him "richly" (Colossians 3:16²).

In this cynical world that asks, "What is truth?" (John 18:38²),
I ask that he "will know the truth" of your teaching, so that
"the truth will set" him "free" (8:32¹)—free to live for you
and know your joy, Jesus!

I pray he will be, like you, a "man of truth" with "nothing false about him" (7:18).

"May integrity and honesty protect" him, because he puts his "hope in you" (Psalm 25:21[1]).

May he be a man who tells the truth when it isn't to his own advantage and who keeps his promises "even when it hurts" (15:4[1]).

Give him insight to see through this world's toxic fog, the deception that says whatever he believes is okay as long as it makes him happy. Only *you* lead to lasting happiness!

I ask that he humbly embrace the beauty of your saving truth with all his heart. May he speak "the truth from" his "heart" (15:2[4]) because you reside there.

When the adversary tries to undermine your truth, fill him afresh with your Spirit. Your Spirit is "the Spirit of truth" whom "the world cannot receive, because it neither sees him nor knows him" (John 14:17[2]). But I pray my son will "know him," because your Spirit "dwells with" him "and will be in" him.

May he be "firmly established in the truth" (2 Peter 1:12) of all you are, Lord!

"I have no greater joy" than to hear that he's "walking in the truth" (3 John 1:4). Come what may, he'll always be safe there—because he is walking with you.

WRAPPED IN RIGHTEOUSNESS

. . . with the breastplate of righteousness in place.

EPHESIANS 6:14

Righteousness is such a challenging thing, Lord.

"What is man . . . that he can be righteous?" (Job 15:14²).

When we make even a little progress, we're so easily tempted to pride ourselves on it. Yet "pride goes before destruction, and a haughty spirit before a fall" (Proverbs 16:18²).

Your Word makes this clear: "Look at the proud! They trust in themselves, and their lives are crooked. But the righteous will live by their faithfulness" to you (Habakkuk 2:4¹).

How can we be righteous without being righteous in our own eyes?

Only through you. You alone are righteous. You are "The LORD Our Righteousness" (Jeremiah 23:6⁵); you "put on righteousness as" *your* "breastplate" (Isaiah 59:17).

So today I pray my daughter will wear "the breastplate of righteousness" (Ephesians 6:14) and wear it right. I pray she'll borrow yours.

She can only do that if you put it on her. She needs "a righteousness" that "comes through faith" in you, Jesus: "the righteousness from God that depends on faith" (Philippians

3:9[2]). Only a "righteousness that is by faith from first to last" (Romans 1:17) will give her the protection she needs.

You have become "our righteousness, holiness and redemption" (1 Corinthians 1:30). So I pray my daughter will be protected from spiritual harm by staying close to you. "The promise" of life is in you (2 Timothy 1:1[2])!

I ask that she may worship you wholeheartedly and completely "rely on" what you've done for her, putting "no confidence in human effort" (Philippians 3:3[1]).

Then you will be all the answer needed to the one "who accuses" her "day and night" (Revelation 12:10). "The body armor" of your righteousness (Ephesians 6:14[1]) will protect her completely!

Thank you for speaking "to the Father for us" (1 John 2:1[4]), Jesus.

I praise you for your priceless righteousness. Please give my daughter wisdom to understand that obedience to you is the only response we can give for your goodness to us.

If she comprehends that, one day you'll replace the strong and shining body armor you've given her with "fine linen, bright and pure"—linen that represents "the righteous deeds of the saints" (Revelation 19:8[2]).

Then, safe and sound at last with the battle won, she'll find herself before you in indescribable joy, at "the wedding feast of the Lamb" (v. 7[1]).

NEW SHOES!

For shoes, put on the peace that comes from the
Good News so that you will be fully prepared.

EPHESIANS 6:15[1]

Today I'm asking for beautiful feet for my child.

Your Word says, "How beautiful are the feet of those who
bring good news!" (Romans 10:15). I pray _____ will
carry your good news wherever he goes. May he love you
so much that he'll be compelled to share you with others in
the things he does and says.

I pray your peace will rest upon him so deeply that he'll "always be prepared to give an answer to everyone who asks"
him to "give the reason for the hope" that he has, and that
he'll "do this with gentleness and respect" (1 Peter 3:15).

When we're little, we get so excited about new shoes. We
believe they'll help us run faster and jump higher. We put
such faith in them! But today I pray that _____ will have
new faith in you so that your strength "powerfully works"
(Colossians 1:29) through him.

May he be someone you're pleased with, someone with a
servant's heart who considers your interests above his own.
Then one day he'll hear you say, "Well done, good and
faithful servant! You have been faithful with a few things; I
will put you in charge of many things. Come and share your
master's happiness!" (Matthew 25:23).

If he walks in your peace, ready to serve you, you will keep him "safe in" your "love" (Jude 1:21[1]).

I pray that he'll stay on your path and "not swerve to the right or the left," so that you keep his "foot away from evil" (Proverbs 4:27[2]).

You came to "guide our feet into the path of peace" (Luke 1:79). Please teach him how to follow you on it!

I ask that he "pursue righteousness and a godly life, along with faith, love, perseverance, and gentleness" (1 Timothy 6:11[1]).

May the wonder of who you are and the peace that you give help him walk into new places of grace, where he sees you at work and praises you for it.

I pray that my son will know the joy of sharing you with others and witness your amazing power to transform hearts and lives.

May you move through him to "say to the captives, 'Come out,' and to those in darkness, 'Be free!'" (Isaiah 49:9).

Then may he watch in wordless wonder as it happens—as chains break, light falls on faces, and hearts turn to you, "God our savior . . . the hope of everyone on earth" (Psalm 65:5[1]).

WHEN BELIEVING IS SEEING

In addition to all this, take up the shield of faith, with which you can extinguish all the flaming arrows of the evil one.

EPHESIANS 6:16

I pray that my child will pick up the shield of faith and use it well.

I see it in her hands now, a strong shield emblazoned with "the Lion of the tribe of Judah" who "has triumphed" (Revelation 5:5).

She is fragile, Jesus—but because she is yours, she conquers! "This is the victory that has overcome the world—our faith" (1 John 5:4[2]).

So by faith I bring her before you and see her standing strong through your mercy.

But I know what she faces: a dark and menacing adversary. His eye is keen and his flaming arrow flies straight at her weakness.

But it misses! In wisdom quicker than thought, your Spirit speaks to her and she obeys—the shield flashes! The arrow glances away and falls broken to the ground.

My child lives! Just as you promised: "Because I live, you will live also" (John 14:19[3]).

You stand "beside" us "like a great warrior" (Jeremiah 20:11[1]), so I pray for your protection for her as long as she must "fight the good fight" of faith (1 Timothy 6:12[2]).

May "your compassion come speedily to meet" her (Psalm 79:8[2]). With you she can "extinguish all the flaming arrows of the evil one" (Ephesians 6:16), regardless of how many come her way.

Strong Savior, you promise such beautiful things to those who believe. You said, "I have come as a light to shine in this dark world, so that all who put their trust in me will no longer remain in the dark" (John 12:46[1]). Let your "light of life" (Job 33:30[2]) shine on her, Lord!

You said, "Anyone who believes in me will live, even after dying" (John 11:25[1]). "Anyone who believes has *eternal* life" (6:47[1]). So I pray she will believe.

You "gave" yourself for her "to redeem" her (Titus 2:14[2]) and set her free "from the power of darkness" (Colossians 1:13[3]). Your Word assures us that "everyone who believes" in you "receives forgiveness of sins" through your "name" (Acts 10:43[2]).

May she "live by faith, not by sight" (2 Corinthians 5:7).

I pray that she may have "the assurance of things hoped for" and "the conviction of things not seen" (Hebrews 11:1[2]) before they even occur, because she "can confidently say, 'The Lord is my helper'" (13:6[2]).

"All things are possible for one who believes" (Mark 9:23[2]), because the One she believes in is *you*!

HELMET OF HOPE

And take the helmet of salvation.

EPHESIANS 6:17[2]

I pray that my child will be "protected by the armor of faith and love," and I ask that you help him put on "the confidence of our salvation" (1 Thessalonians 5:8[1]) as a helmet.

Our adversary the devil is a predator and "the father of lies" (John 8:44). "When anyone hears the message about the kingdom and does not understand it, the evil one comes and snatches away what was sown in their heart" (Matthew 13:19).

So I ask that you fill my son with an extra measure of spiritual "wisdom and understanding" (Colossians 1:9[4]).

I pray that he will "be on guard" and "stand firm in the faith," and that he will learn to "be courageous" and "strong" (1 Corinthians 16:13[1]).

When the devil tries to assault his mind and attack what he believes, I pray he will keep his "head in all situations" (2 Timothy 4:5).

May there be no doubt in his mind that you have saved him, Jesus. May he praise you for "such a great salvation" (Hebrews 2:3[2])!

Just as Abraham "believed" you and was called your "friend" (James 2:23[2]), I pray my son will have a deep relationship with you that will empower him daily. Then he will "not lose heart" regardless of his external circumstances, because "inwardly" he is "being renewed day by day" (2 Corinthians 4:16).

May he be able to say with great confidence, "I know the one in whom I trust, and I am sure that he is able to guard what I have entrusted to him" (2 Timothy 1:12[1]).

Assure him of his faith so that he will be able to pray, "You have been my hope, Sovereign LORD," and "my confidence since my youth" (Psalm 71:5).

You have promised, Lord Jesus, that "the gates of hell shall not prevail" against your church (Matthew 16:18[2]). May he be so strong in you and in your "mighty power" (Ephesians 6:10) that he will join your church in the assault on those gates. May the sheer force of your strength in him cause the gates to shudder, setting captives free!

I pray my son will be active in "sharing" his faith (Philemon 1:6[3]), so that he "will completely understand every good thing" we have in you (v. 6[4]).

Then he will love you "even though" he has "never seen" you and will "rejoice with a glorious, inexpressible joy" (1 Peter 1:8[1]).

May "the hope laid up" for him "in heaven" protect him from head to toe (Colossians 1:5[2]), until the battle is done and the victory is yours forever.

PROTECTED BY YOUR WORD

Take . . . the sword of the Spirit, which is the word of God.

EPHESIANS 6:17

Today I pray the power of your Word over my child's life.

You use your Word "to prepare and equip" us "to do every good work" (2 Timothy 3:17[1]), so I pray the wisdom of your Word will protect my child as long as he lives.

I pray that your Word will be "hidden" in his heart so he "might not sin against you" (Psalm 119:11).

"All Scripture is inspired" by you, "useful to teach us what is true and to make us realize what is wrong in our lives. It corrects us . . . and teaches us to do what is right" (2 Timothy 3:16[1]).

Jesus, every time the devil tempted you in the wilderness, you answered, "It is written . . ." (Matthew 4:4, 7, 10[2]). I pray that when the devil tries to lead my child astray, you will help him find his answer and "way of escape" (1 Corinthians 10:13[5]) through your Word.

Your Word "is alive and powerful. It is sharper than the sharpest two-edged sword, cutting between soul and spirit, between joint and marrow" (Hebrews 4:12[1]).

Let your Word protect him! Guide his steps "by your word," so he "will not be overcome by evil" (Psalm 119:133[1]).

I ask that my son will be a man "who correctly handles the word of truth" (2 Timothy 2:15). Let him know it and understand it well.

When the world around him insists on going its own way, may he not "wander from the truth" (James 5:19) or "neglect your word" (Psalm 119:16). Help him not to "be wise" in his own "estimation" (Romans 12:16[5]) by valuing human wisdom above your own.

May he respect your Word and even "stand in awe" of it (Psalm 119:120[1]).

Because the Bible points him to you, let him say, "How I love your instructions! I think about them all day long" (v. 97[1]).

Your Spirit speaks through your Word unlike anywhere else. Let him long to spend time with you there, to hear your voice and know the comfort that you give.

I pray "your word" will be his "source of hope" (v. 114[1]), a refreshing place of encouragement for his soul.

Open his eyes "to see the wonderful truths in your instructions" (v. 18[1]). May your Word be his "treasure" and his "heart's delight" (v. 111[1])!

"Heaven and earth will pass away," but your words "will never pass away" (Mark 13:31).

Lifted by your "Spirit of truth" (John 15:26[2]), may his heart leap from the page and soar to the perfect peace of your presence.

ARMORED WITH PRAYER

And pray in the Spirit on all occasions with all kinds
of prayers and requests. With this in mind, be alert and
always keep on praying for all the Lord's people.

EPHESIANS 6:18

May _____ discover the blessing of prayer, Father. All the
armor you give is to help us pray!

Prayer is more than just armor—it's a gift that welcomes
you into our lives.

"The weapons we fight with are not the weapons of the
world. On the contrary, they have divine power to demolish
strongholds" (2 Corinthians 10:4).

Help my daughter to comprehend the power and peace that's
available to us when we pray. You allow our prayers to move
your "mighty hand" (1 Kings 8:42[2])!

Give her insight to understand that some things will happen
"only by prayer" (Mark 9:29).

You wait for us to pray! You've told us, "Call to me and I
will answer you and tell you great and unsearchable things
you do not know" (Jeremiah 33:3).

May she call on you and discover what you can do. Help
her to "devote" herself "to prayer with an alert mind and a
thankful heart" (Colossians 4:2[1]).

Please don't let her be distracted into a busy life where she thinks it's all up to her. Don't let prayer be a last resort in her life. Let it be her first!

May she call on your name "every day" and "spread out" her "hands to you" (Psalm 88:9). May she pray with faith and trust that you "will answer" (Isaiah 30:19).

Abba, thank you that you don't always give us what we ask for. You respond to our prayers with perfect, loving wisdom.

When answers don't come quickly or the way she wants, help her to know that you are our peace. You are "a faithful God," and "those who wait" for your help are always "blessed" (v. 18[1]).

Thank you for the privilege of prayer, Jesus! Thank you for opening a "new and living way" (Hebrews 10:20[2]) into the very presence of the Father.

I praise you that we can "have confidence to enter the Most Holy Place" (v. 19) through your mercy to us on the cross.

Thank you that we can "come boldly to the throne of grace" and "obtain mercy and find grace to help in time of need" (4:16[3]).

May the cry of her heart always be, "I call to God, and the LORD saves me" (Psalm 55:16).

Help her to "pray in the Spirit on all occasions with all kinds of prayers and requests" (Ephesians 6:18), so that she may discover the wonder of all that you are. And help me to "always keep on praying" for her!

FAITHFUL

Gabriel's Lesson

God brings His purposes to pass in spite of all men
may do, and often through what they do, and He
will utilise the very things which look as if they
were going dead against their fulfilment; God goes
steadily on and involves us in the fulfilment.

OSWALD CHAMBERS

It's a lesson in prayer from the mouth of an angel, and it comes when you least expect it.

Elizabeth and Zechariah had prayed for a baby for years. But year after year, the prayer seemed to go unanswered. Or maybe God's answer was "No."

Some began to wonder why. Having no children was a "disgrace" in their opinion (Luke 1:25), a sign that someone had displeased God. So neighbors and "friends" began to speculate that maybe God was judging Elizabeth and Zechariah for some secret sin.

The years went by until Zechariah and Elizabeth "were both very old" (v. 7[1]). One day, Zechariah was on duty in the temple. He was standing alone in the sanctuary when none other than the archangel Gabriel appeared.

The old man was terrified, but Gabriel told him, "Don't be afraid, Zechariah! God has heard your prayer. Your wife, Elizabeth, will give you a son, and you are to name him John. You will have great joy and gladness, and many will rejoice at his birth, for he will be great in the eyes of the Lord" (vv. 13–15[1]).

There it is: Gabriel's lesson. Did you catch it? Like so many things that angels do, it happened so quickly that it's easy to miss. The lesson is found in five little words: *God has heard your prayer.*

If you were Zechariah, you might be wondering, *What prayer?* Elizabeth's childbearing years were long past. It's doubtful Zechariah had in mind the answer to a request made decades earlier.

But as soon as Gabriel saw Zechariah, that was one of the first things out of his mouth. And there's comfort in that for every praying parent.

God's timing is rarely our own, but it is always perfect. We may ask for good things for our children—things that we know God would want us to pray for—but we don't always see them happening. That doesn't mean blessings won't come. We can still trust that good will occur, even if we don't know how or when. Our part is to rest and trust in God, knowing that He is faithful to remember our prayers even if we made them years earlier, and that He himself is the best answer to prayer before and after any other answer comes, because His "grace is sufficient" (2 Corinthians 12:9).

Sometimes God doesn't give us what we seek when we ask for it because He's waiting to give us something better. Zechariah and Elizabeth longed for a son—but God gave them a prophet. And not just any prophet. They got a man with "the spirit and power of Elijah" (Luke 1:17)—the very one who would announce the Messiah.

The pages to come are filled with prayers that our children will have faith in God and discover His faithfulness for themselves. There are practical prayers about confidence in God, personal integrity, the meaning of true success, obedience, "moving mountains," and more.

As you pray these prayers, I hope you'll take Gabriel's lesson to heart. God hears our prayers! Zechariah and Elizabeth may have lost faith that their prayers would ever be answered. But God didn't. He was only taking His perfect time, preparing a miracle.

MUSTARD SEEDS, MOUNTAINS, AND PROMISED LANDS

I tell you the truth, if you had faith even as small as a mustard seed, you could say to this mountain, "Move from here to there," and it would move. Nothing would be impossible.

MATTHEW 17:20[1]

Sometimes my son will have to face mountains.

So I pray for those faith-building moments when he must choose to "trust in" you (Psalm 115:9[2]).

I'm reminded of Joshua and Caleb. When Moses sent a team to scout out the land you promised to your people, Joshua and Caleb were the only ones who believed they could overcome the obstacles. They told the people not to "be afraid" and assured them that you were with them (Numbers 14:9).

But the people didn't believe. So you said, "Not one of them will ever see the land I promised" (v. 23). Only Joshua and Caleb got to go in.

Father, I don't want _____ to miss what you've promised!

Help me to do my part to "see to it" that my child does not have "a sinful, unbelieving heart that turns away" from you, "the living God" (Hebrews 3:12).

When others around him doubt, please give him a "different spirit" so that he "follows" you "wholeheartedly" (Numbers

14:24). May he receive many blessings because he believes in you!

You are "a rewarder of those who diligently seek" you (Hebrews 11:6[3]).

Even though obstacles may stand before him, in your presence "the mountains quake, and the hills melt away" (Nahum 1:5[1]).

So I pray he'll stand with you. As long as his faith is in you, "nothing will be impossible" (Matthew 17:20[2]).

Help him to look beyond life's challenges and see you. Give him faith to understand that you're greater than anything he faces.

I pray he'll walk so closely with you that he'll have the "confidence" you give, quietly assured that you will answer his prayers because he's asking "according to" your will (1 John 5:14).

You are "the great God, the mighty and awesome God" (Deuteronomy 10:17[1]) who works miracles! You are "the only one who is worthy" of praise (v. 21[1]).

So I pray he'll enjoy praising you often. The more he praises you, the more his faith will grow.

Even a little faith—just a mustard seed—is a powerful thing when placed in your hands. I ask that he may "look to" you and your "strength," and "seek" your "face always" (1 Chronicles 16:11), until the day that he joyfully enters the "better country—a heavenly one"—that you have waiting for him (Hebrews 11:16)!

"YOU CAN DO IT!"

Then Moses said, "If you don't personally go with us,
don't make us leave this place." . . . The LORD replied
to Moses, "I will indeed do what you have asked, for I
look favorably on you, and I know you by name."

EXODUS 33:15, 17[1]

How you honored Moses, Lord!

He was given a special place in history for leading your people.

Your Word shows us what made him great and the reason you
singled him out: "Moses was a very humble man, more humble
than anyone else on the face of the earth" (Numbers 12:3).

Moses had the confidence to lead a nation out of slavery
against incredible odds because his confidence wasn't in
himself. It was in you.

I ask for the same confidence for _____, Lord.

When he faces challenges in life, I pray he will "not be afraid
or discouraged," because he understands that "the battle" is
not his but yours (2 Chronicles 20:15).

This can only happen if he lives for you and walks with you.

May he live in such a way that you "look favorably on" him
(Exodus 33:17[1])! Like Moses, may he hear your voice quietly
assuring him, "I know you by name."

I pray for great faith in my child's life, a faith with vision
to grasp that "what is impossible with man is possible with
God" (Luke 18:27[2]).

"Through faith" in you, Lord Jesus, "we may approach God with freedom and confidence" (Ephesians 3:12). I pray that he will!

I pray you will "personally go with" him (Exodus 33:15[1]) wherever he goes, so that he may be blessed with an awareness of your presence.

How blessed we are when we know you and our thoughts are filled with you.

May he watch and listen for your leading, longing to please you. When the world tells him it can't be done, may he hear you say, "You can do it in my strength!"

Your Word makes clear that "those who trust their own insight are foolish" (Proverbs 28:26[1]). But if we trust in you, all will be well, no matter what.

"Such confidence" is ours through you, Lord Jesus, because "our competence comes from God" (2 Corinthians 3:4–5).

May he live a righteous, faithful life because he is in love with you. Then "the fruit of that righteousness will be peace" in his heart before you, and "its effect will be quietness and confidence forever" (Isaiah 32:17).

"Nothing is too hard for you" (Jeremiah 32:17[2])! You are "El-Shaddai—'God Almighty'" (Genesis 35:11[1]).

And if he holds on to "confidence" in you, he "will be richly rewarded" (Hebrews 10:35).

WORK OF YOUR HANDS

The LORD has filled Bezalel with the Spirit of God,
giving him great wisdom, ability, and expertise in
all kinds of crafts. He is a master craftsman.

EXODUS 35:31–32[1]

What is it you want _____ to do, Lord?

Samuel was young when you called him. So was David. And John the Baptist hadn't even been born yet (Luke 1:5–25)!

But your Spirit was at work in them, helping them accomplish just what you wanted them to do in life.

I pray this for my child as well, and I ask that you use me to encourage him in his life's work.

But I also pray you will help me not to force my will or my way on him. "We can make our plans," but you determine "our steps" (Proverbs 16:9[1]).

May "your will be done" (Matthew 6:10) in his life and work!

I pray he will follow you into whatever work you have planned for him.

When he is trying to determine what he should do, I pray that he will "ask" you "for guidance" (Isaiah 8:19[1]), and that you will make the way so clear that he cannot miss it.

Please give him wisdom to understand that his work is a calling and gift from you. "Whatever" he does, may he "work at it with all" his "heart," as someone "working for" you (Colossians 3:23), not for himself.

May his work be *your* work, Jesus! May you move through him to accomplish beautiful things.

Just as you were "with Joseph and gave him success in whatever he did" (Genesis 39:23), I ask that you show _____ favor.

Should he be blessed with things, I pray he "would never say" to himself, "I have achieved this wealth with my own strength and energy" (Deuteronomy 8:17[1]).

May he understand that you are "the one who gives" us "power to be successful" (v. 18[1]). Any ability we have—including the strength to apply it—is a gift from you.

Please keep him from the idolatry of self and things, Father!

May he see money as your tool in his hands to further your work and bless others. May he bring "the whole tithe" into your house, so you will "throw open the floodgates of heaven and pour out so much blessing that there will not be room enough to store it" (Malachi 3:10).

May he use his "worldly resources to benefit others" (Luke 16:8[1]) so that they come to know you.

And when his work on earth is done, I pray he will hear you say, "Well done, good and faithful servant! You have been faithful with a few things; I will put you in charge of many things. Come and share your master's happiness!" (Matthew 25:23).

WHEN NO ONE IS LOOKING

Remember, the sins of some people are obvious, leading
them to certain judgment. But there are others whose
sins will not be revealed until later. In the same way, the
good deeds of some people are obvious. And the good
deeds done in secret will someday come to light.

1 TIMOTHY 5:24–25[1]

I pray that _____ will have the integrity to do what is
right when no one is looking.

You are always watching, Father! You see us even when we
think no one does.

We "can never escape from your Spirit!" (Psalm 139:7[1]). We
"can never get away from your presence!"

"You spread out our sins before you—our secret sins—and
you see them all" (90:8[1]).

But because you see all of "what is done in secret," you also
"reward" us when we are faithful to you (Matthew 6:4). So
I pray that she will be.

I ask that you continually remind her of your presence so
she may be comforted and encouraged when she is alone.

I pray that she will be compelled by your Spirit to do what
is right because she understands that you are her constant
companion and closest friend.

When people *are* watching, may she do what is right out of love for you—not to be "admired by others," so that she won't "lose the reward" you have waiting for her (v. 1[1]).

Please also give her favor with others so that her life has an impact for you. Your Word tells us that "a good name is more desirable than great riches," and "to be esteemed is better than silver or gold" (Proverbs 22:1).

Help her to have integrity, Jesus. "The integrity of the upright guides them" (11:3[2]). "People with integrity walk safely, but those who follow crooked paths will be exposed" (10:9[1]).

When her road is uphill, I pray she will continue to trust you to show yourself faithful.

You "personally rescued" your people again and again, and "lifted them up and carried them through all the years" (Isaiah 63:9[1]). May the sweetness of your Spirit give her what she needs to happily choose your way above any other.

And when she is tempted, may she choose you then too.

Our ways are in your "full view," Father (Proverbs 5:21). And one day, you "will bring to light what is hidden in darkness and will expose the motives" of our hearts (1 Corinthians 4:5).

Even "the good deeds done in secret will someday come to light" (1 Timothy 5:25[1]). When all is revealed, may her actions show that she loves you most of all!

TENDING THE TEMPLE

Do you not know that your bodies are temples of the
Holy Spirit, who is in you, whom you have received
from God? You are not your own; you were bought
at a price. Therefore honor God with your bodies.

1 CORINTHIANS 6:19–20

I pray that _____ will take good care of herself, Lord.
Not just for her benefit—I pray she'll do it for you. May she
"honor" you with her body (1 Corinthians 6:20).

What amazing bodies you've given us!

We are "fearfully and wonderfully made; your works are
wonderful" (Psalm 139:14).

You are so good to take the things we need to do to stay
alive—like eating and drinking—and make them pleasurable.

Every sense we may have been blessed with—taste, touch,
sight, smell, hearing—is a gift from you. May she never take
these gifts for granted, and thank you for every one she has.

Let her marvel at them, using them to praise you for even the
smallest blessings of flavor, sound, color, aroma, or texture.

Help her understand how deeply you care "about our bodies"
(1 Corinthians 6:13[1]). "Even the hairs" of our heads "are all
numbered" (Luke 12:7[2])!

May she also understand that her body is "a temple" of your Holy Spirit (1 Corinthians 6:19²).

May she exercise and eat right, not out of vanity but from gratitude. May she take care of all you've blessed her with so she may serve you effectively.

I pray she'll have emotional maturity and self-control with her body, so that she "will not be mastered by anything" (v. 12).

Please give her wisdom to "flee from sexual immorality," because "the sexually immoral person sins against his own body" (v. 18²).

Protect her also from pressure in our culture to look a certain way. Help her understand that her body is beautiful simply because you made her the way she is, and she is the work of your hands.

I pray that "the excitement of youth" will not cause her "to forget" you, her Creator (Ecclesiastes 12:1¹).

When she's healthy and strong, may she know you are "enabling" her "to stand on mountain heights" (Psalm 18:33¹).

When she's sick, may she know you as "the LORD who heals" (Exodus 15:26¹).

Whatever her condition, may she always know you!

Then, when her life on earth is done and the "last trumpet" sounds and she is "raised imperishable," we'll praise you together, saying, "Thanks be to God, who gives us the victory through our Lord Jesus Christ" (1 Corinthians 15:52, 57²)!

RESPONSIBLE

And the Lord replied, "A faithful, sensible servant is
one to whom the master can give the responsibility of
managing his other household servants and feeding
them. If the master returns and finds that the servant
has done a good job, there will be a reward."

LUKE 12:42–43[1]

Please help my son to learn what it means to be responsible,
Lord Jesus.

I pray he will be someone who can be trusted to carry out
even the smallest task.

If he knows how to be "faithful in little things," he will be
"faithful in large ones" (Luke 16:10[1]).

Help him understand that if he compromises, you will notice . . . even though others may not.

When you told the parable about the "faithful, sensible servant," it was about so much more than earthly "responsibility" (12:42[1]). You said that if we are "untrustworthy about
worldly wealth," we won't be able to handle "the true riches
of heaven" (16:11[1]). This is a kingdom thing!

So I pray _____ will prepare for your kingdom and look
for it to "come soon" (11:2[1]).

Whether he's cleaning his room, completing an exam, or filling
out a tax return, please help him to be honest and faithful to
you. You promised "a reward" for those who are (12:43[1])!

Please protect him from the ungodly influence of "those of this world whose reward is in this life" (Psalm 17:14). "Evil people get rich for the moment, but the reward of the godly will last" (Proverbs 11:18[1]).

Help him remember that he is living for so much more than this world. "Each person is destined to die once and after that comes judgment" (Hebrews 9:27[1]).

You told us that "a time is coming when all who are in their graves" will hear your voice "and come out"—and "those who have done what is good will rise to live" (John 5:28–29). I want him to live forever in your kingdom, Jesus!

May he be among those who look forward to your kingdom without "looking back" (Luke 9:62[3]). You are "not ashamed to be called their God," and you have "prepared a city for them" (Hebrews 11:16).

Beyond any reward, I pray he will simply look forward to *you*.

I pray that he will love you for who you are, not just for what you can do for him. Please help him to seek your face and not just your hand.[7]

When he thinks of all that is to come and all you've promised, may he think of you most of all. You are the best Reward, because you are the one who makes it heaven!

THAT ALL
MAY GO WELL

Children, obey your parents because you belong to the Lord,
for this is the right thing to do. "Honor your father and
mother." This is the first commandment with a promise:
If you honor your father and mother, "things will go well
for you, and you will have a long life on the earth."

EPHESIANS 6:1–3[1]

I want my daughter to be so blessed, Father. And you can
best determine how that happens.

Sometimes when I say I want what's best for her, I'm reminded
of how easy it is for me to see "things merely from a human
point of view" and not from yours (Matthew 16:23[1]).

But your Word reveals the right direction. "Things will go
well" for my child (Ephesians 6:3[1]) if both of us obey and
honor you.

If I don't "do what is right," "love mercy," and "walk humbly"
with you (Micah 6:8[1]), I'll make it difficult for her to
honor or obey me.

How could I expect her to honor the dishonorable or obey
the disobedient?

So I pray that you will help me to live an exemplary life
before her, a life that lovingly points to you.

May she see you in me, Jesus, and be drawn to you, "the
Shepherd" of her soul (1 Peter 2:25[2]).

You know what we're up against, Lord. The "rebellion" of our world lays "heavy upon it" (Isaiah 24:20).

In a world that does not honor you, it would be easier for my child to go with the flow and rebel at times. But I ask that you protect her from "the spirit who is now at work in those who are disobedient" (Ephesians 2:2) and help her "not conform to the pattern of this world" (Romans 12:2).

I pray she will be an original—your original!

May she want to "respect" her "mother and father" (Leviticus 19:3[1]) because she wants to honor and obey *you*. You promised she will be blessed if she does!

Help her to "show proper respect to everyone" (1 Peter 2:17). May a healthy respect for authority be part of her life.

May she "give to everyone" what they are owed: "taxes and government fees to those who collect them" and "respect and honor to those who are in authority" (Romans 13:7[1]).

But may she honor your authority most of all.

You tell us that "those who love your instructions have great peace and do not stumble" (Psalm 119:165[1]). I want that for her, because this is about love. Love that inspires her to live with purpose for something much larger than herself—you!

May she always be "aware of your unfailing love" and live "according to your truth" (26:3[1]).

WEEK 7

FRUITFUL

The Mess and the Message

Bestow, dear Lord, upon our youth,
The gift of saving grace;
And let the seed of sacred truth
Fall in a fruitful place.

WILLIAM COWPER

God has a way of planting the most fruitful seeds where we may not see them. Some of the most difficult circumstances of our lives become fertile ground for growth we never expected and fruit that could not have come any other way.

God wastes nothing. He is even able to take what the adversary meant for evil and turn it to good, "the saving of many lives" (Genesis 50:20). Nowhere did this become more apparent in my own life than in our son's struggle with substance abuse.

Our son went through a heartbreaking season that lasted seven years. God eventually set Geoff free from a severe addiction and is using him powerfully today in a ministry that helps those who wrestle in similar ways. He has a unique, hard-won ability to understand what others are going through and to share the difference Jesus has made in his life in a winsome, nonjudgmental way. When I asked Geoff if he minded if I shared the change God had made in his life, his response was, "Dad, I want you to tell it. I *prefer* that you tell my story, because it's pointless if others don't hear about it. Why else would God have done it?"

Baseball great Darryl Strawberry shares that perspective. After earning eight all-star selections and four World Series rings, his brilliant seventeen-year career was ruined by addiction. But then Jesus saved him and set him free. Since then, Strawberry has dedicated his life to ministering to other athletes caught in the web he once knew. He summed up God's transformation of his life with these words: "Here I am, a baseball superstar, falling into the pits, having everybody write you off and then having God say, 'I'm going to use your mess for a message.' How beautiful is that?"[8]

Where God's Spirit is at work, beautiful fruit can grow from the same ground where there was once only decay. So this week we are boldly praying for the fruit of the Spirit in our children's lives: "love, joy, peace, patience, kindness, goodness, faithfulness, gentleness, and self-control" (Galatians 5:22–23[1]).

God deeply desires to bring all of these things into our children's hearts as they live for Him. Pray with faith! He is able to use our prayers to plant seeds even where there's a mess. And the message that grows there will be for His glory.

"I LOVE YOU, DADDY"

The fruit of the Spirit is love.

GALATIANS 5:22

I love you, O Lᴏʀᴅ, my strength.

PSALM 18:1[2]

I love to hear _____ tell me, "I love you." So I want to tell *you* the same thing.

I love you, Lord, and I praise you for the beautiful blessing of being a parent.

Having a child I love so much teaches me about your heart and how much you love us.

It shows me the incredible depth of your sacrifice, Father. You did not "spare" your "own Son but gave him up for us all" (Romans 8:32[2]), because you love *us* so much!

I cannot imagine the pain you went through on our behalf.

Jesus, I praise you that your life-giving sacrifice for us on the cross is "accomplished" (Luke 12:50[2]), and that you have gone "to the Father" and have "loved" your own "to the end" (John 13:1). You will "reign forever and ever" (Revelation 11:15[1])!

How can we not love you for all you have done for us?

"We know that we live" in you and you live in us, because you have also "given us" your "Spirit" (1 John 4:13). And your Spirit draws us close to you.

We "have not received a spirit that makes" us "fearful slaves" (Romans 8:15[1]). We "received" your Spirit when you "adopted" us as your "own children." So "now we" can even "call" you "Abba, Father"—another way of saying "Daddy!"

Abba, I pray _____ will give you the joy of saying, "I love you, Daddy," not just with words but through *living* intentionally for you.

I pray that she will "love" you with all her "heart," "soul," and "mind" (Matthew 22:37[2]).

May she love you with all she is and live each day expectantly in your presence.

Because of your tender "mercies," may she fully give herself to you "as a living sacrifice, holy and acceptable" (Romans 12:1[2]). May she be devoted to you, even understanding that honoring you with her body is "spiritual worship."

I pray that the "fruit of the Spirit" will abound in her, especially the first one: "love" (Galatians 5:22). May she love you more than self—more even than life—understanding that you "graciously give us all things" (Romans 8:32)!

"What shall we say" about the "wonderful things" you have done for us and will continue to do (v. 31[1])? If you are for us, "who can ever be against us?"

So I'll say it again.

"I love you, O LORD, my strength" (Psalm 18:1[2]). And I pray my child will love you too!

STRONG IN JOY

But the fruit of the Spirit is . . . joy.

GALATIANS 5:22

Don't be dejected and sad, for the joy
of the LORD is your strength!

NEHEMIAH 8:10[1]

Thank you for the joy you give, Father. There's nothing like it!

Your joy is alive, the result of your "Spirit living within" us (Romans 8:11[1]). Your Word tells us that just as you "raised Christ Jesus from the dead," you "will give life" even to our "mortal bodies" because your Spirit lives in us.

"How precious to me are your thoughts, God!" (Psalm 139:17).

You save us and make us new, giving us life from the inside out.

You are joy, Lord Jesus! How can we ever have deep and lasting happiness apart from you?

So I pray _____ will know the joy you give because he genuinely knows *you.*

May he have a close and tender relationship with you that gives him daily access to inexhaustible joy—joy that is more than a feeling.

Help him to take the steps he needs to take to walk into your joy every day.

I pray he will learn to praise you even when it isn't easy. When Nehemiah told the people of Israel to choose joy, he told them not to "be dejected and sad," because your "joy" was their "strength" (Nehemiah 8:10[1]).

When David was going through difficulty, he told you, "My heart is confident in you, O God; my heart is confident. No wonder I can sing your praises! Wake up, my heart!" (Psalm 57:7–8[1]).

I ask that you awaken my son's heart to the wonder and strength of all that you are.

May he be determined to praise you, just like David when he said, "I *will* praise you, LORD, with all my heart; I *will* tell of all the marvelous things you have done. I *will* be filled with joy because of you. I *will* sing praises to your name, O Most High" (9:1–2[1]).

I pray your joy will overflow from my son's heart into the lives of others. May your "joy" be in him so his "joy may be complete" (John 15:11)!

Please give him wisdom to stay away from the sadness of sin and its "fleeting pleasures" (Hebrews 11:25[2]).

You can give us *true* bliss. Only "you will show" him "the way of life," granting him "the joy of your presence and the pleasures of living with you forever" (Psalm 16:11[1]).

May the fruit of your joy grow and mature in my child's life, Lord Jesus, so that he becomes an example of pure happiness in you!

ANTI-ANXIETY

But the fruit of the Spirit is . . . peace.

GALATIANS 5:22

You will keep in perfect peace all who trust in
you, all whose thoughts are fixed on you!

ISAIAH 26:3[1]

I praise you for your peace, Jesus.

You are the "Prince of Peace" (Isaiah 9:6[2]), and you promise
"peace" to your "people" (Psalm 85:8).

You told us, "I am leaving you with a gift—peace of mind
and heart. And the peace I give is a gift the world cannot
give. So don't be troubled or afraid" (John 14:27[1]).

I pray that _____ will live with your peace in her heart,
Lord.

This can only happen if she walks with you, for that path is
where "happiness is found" (Psalm 119:35[1]).

Help her understand that her salvation is found in "repentance and rest" in you (Isaiah 30:15), and that you'll give
her fresh strength as she quietly trusts in you.

May she rest in your wisdom for her life and understand that
your ways are "pleasant ways," and that all of your "paths
are peace" (Proverbs 3:17). "A heart at peace" even "gives
life to the body" (14:30)!

May she have wisdom beyond her years to see through the world's counterfeit comforts and to comprehend that "there is no peace" apart from you (Isaiah 48:22).

Please bless my child with friends who set an example of what it's like to live in your peace. May she "look at those who are honest and good" and learn from them, because "a wonderful future awaits those who love peace" (Psalm 37:37[1]).

I pray that she *will* love peace! May she love being near you and have a hunger for your peace that keeps her coming back to you and your Word.

May she understand that your peace for her was hard won, Jesus, and that we only "have peace with God" (Romans 5:1) through your "blood, shed on the cross" (Colossians 1:20).

Because of this, may she "make every effort to be found spotless, blameless and at peace" with you (2 Peter 3:14), and to live "a life of goodness and peace and joy" in the strength that comes through your Holy Spirit (Romans 14:17[1]).

May your peace "rule" in her heart (Colossians 3:15[2])!

I pray that you, "the Lord of peace," will give my child "peace at all times and in every way" (2 Thessalonians 3:16).

May you, "the God of peace, sanctify" her "through and through" (1 Thessalonians 5:23). May her "whole spirit, soul and body be kept blameless" at the day of your return, Lord Jesus. I praise you because you are "faithful," and you will "do it" (v. 24)!

A BETTER REST

But the fruit of the Spirit is . . . patience.

GALATIANS 5:22[2]

We also pray that you will be strengthened with all
his glorious power so you will have all the endurance
and patience you need. May you be filled with joy.

COLOSSIANS 1:11[1]

Teach _____ the secret of patience, Lord.

Help him to understand that patience is learned by resting
in you.

We always need patience when we wait for something; may
he wait for *you* most of all!

I pray the cry of his heart will be, "I wait for the LORD, my
soul waits, and in his word I hope" (Psalm 130:5[2]).

If his heart is set on you, everything else will be placed in
perspective. He can face life with a thankful heart knowing
"all things" are his already (1 Corinthians 3:21[2]), because you
have "enabled" him "to share in the inheritance" that belongs
to your "people, who live in the light" (Colossians 1:12[1]).

I pray _____ "will be strengthened" with all the "glorious
power" you give, so that he "will have all the endurance and
patience" he needs (v. 11[1]).

Holy Spirit, please fill him with your loving presence, so he
may "be joyful in hope, patient in affliction," and "faithful
in prayer" (Romans 12:12).

Whenever he has to wait, may he learn to fill the moments by turning to you in prayer.

Our world wants everything yesterday. But your Word says, "Wait for the LORD and keep *his* way, and he will exalt you" (Psalm 37:34²). So may he "be strong and take heart and wait" for you (27:14), looking for your will and way above his own.

When things happen that try his patience, help him to learn the contentment of your company.

Help him say with David, "I have calmed and quieted my soul" (131:2²).

No matter how badly he wants something, may he find peace with this thought: "Return to your rest, my soul, for the LORD has been good to you" (116:7).

"Whoever is patient has great understanding" (Proverbs 14:29), and "knowledge of" you, "the Holy One *is* understanding" (9:10).

"Better to be patient than powerful; better to have self-control than to conquer a city" (16:32¹).

May his strength be in you! May he walk in "all humility and gentleness, with patience, bearing with" others "in love" (Ephesians 4:2²).

You have such beautiful patience with us, Lord, and I pray he'll learn from you. May he stay so close to you that your patience shines through him!

GRACE-FULL

But the fruit of the Spirit is . . . kindness, goodness.

GALATIANS 5:22

And God is able to make all grace abound to you,
so that having all sufficiency in all things at all
times, you may abound in every good work.

2 CORINTHIANS 9:8[2]

I praise you for your amazing grace to us, Father.

When we were "dead" in our "transgressions and sins" (Ephesians 2:1), you showed incredible "kindness to us in Christ Jesus" (v. 7).

You "canceled the record of the charges against us and took it away by nailing it to the cross" (Colossians 2:14[1]).

In your "great mercy" you even gave "us new birth into a living hope through the resurrection of Jesus Christ from the dead" (1 Peter 1:3).

You "forgave us all our sins" and made us "alive with Christ" (Colossians 2:13)—and you didn't have to do it!

But you did it because you are *so good*. You held nothing back from us, not even your only Son.

You keep on giving to us in every way. You even "make all grace abound" to us, so that "in all things at all times," we may "abound in every good work" (2 Corinthians 9:8[2]).

I pray that _____ may have "life by the power" of your name (John 20:31[1]), a relationship "filled with the fruit of righteousness that comes through" you "to the glory and praise of God" (Philippians 1:11).

"Your compassion, LORD, is great" (Psalm 119:156), and I ask that she be filled with it.

Fill her with grace, Abba.

May your love pour from her soul because she is filled to overflowing with your Spirit. Where your Spirit is, "there is freedom" (2 Corinthians 3:17[2])—freedom to grow in the hope that lives within us and boldness to share you with others.

I pray that _____ will bear as "much fruit" (John 15:8[2]) for you as she possibly can, Jesus. May your "kindness" and "goodness" (Galatians 5:22) be one of the first things others see in her!

"You, LORD, are good" (Psalm 25:7), and you "will never stop doing good" for your people (Jeremiah 32:40). Thank you that you will never stop doing good for her, Lord!

You are so kind to us, and I pray my child will "continue to trust" in your "kindness" (Romans 11:22[1]) day after day. May your kindness to her be her inspiration for having compassion for others.

One day, you "will give eternal life to those who keep on doing good" (2:6–7[1]). I ask that she will never "get tired of doing what is good," so that she may "reap a harvest of blessing" (Galatians 6:9[1])!

FAITHFUL FOR LIFE

But the fruit of the Spirit is . . . faithfulness.

GALATIANS 5:22

Where you go I will go, and where you stay I will stay.
Your people will be my people and your God my God.

RUTH 1:16

You blessed Ruth for her faithfulness, Father.

When she chose to stay with Naomi instead of an easier life, you provided for all her needs.

When Ruth told Naomi, "Your God will be my God" (Ruth 1:16[1]) even though she was from Moab and not from Israel, you became her God and gave her "a future hope" (Proverbs 23:18).

You not only blessed her during her lifetime—you blessed her for generations to come. Matthew records her name in the lineage of kings, including David and Solomon and even Jesus (Matthew 1:1–16). How you love faithfulness, Lord!

You are "a faithful God who does no wrong" (Deuteronomy 32:4).

How faithful you are to do what you say and receive us! When we were "living apart from Christ," we were "excluded" from your people and "without hope" (Ephesians 2:12[1]). But now we "can come" to you "through the same Holy Spirit because of what Christ has done for us (v. 18[1]).

I pray that _____ will grow in the faithfulness that your Spirit gives to those who sincerely walk with you.

May she learn faithfulness from you, "the faithful Holy One" (Hosea 11:12).

"To the faithful you show yourself faithful," and "to those with integrity you show integrity" (2 Samuel 22:26[1]).

So I pray she'll "search for faithful people" to be her "companions" (Psalm 101:6[1]) and enjoy the company of those who love and know you.

Help her to be a faithful friend to others, and to you!

Please give her strength to be faithful whether times are good or difficult, because you "will not forsake" your "faithful ones" (37:28).

May she turn to you with "ears wide open" and "listen" to "find life" (Isaiah 55:3[1]). Then she will know "all the unfailing love" you have "promised," all of her life and beyond!

If she is a "faithful and wise servant," she will be "blessed" on the day you return (Matthew 24:45–46[2]).

Please help her to "always want to obey you," and inspire in her a "love for you" that "never changes" (1 Chronicles 29:18[1]).

You are "faithful in all" you do (Psalm 33:4), Father, so please make _____ brave and strong and true!

Then she'll "remain faithful even when facing death," and you who never fail us "will give" her "the crown of life" (Revelation 2:10[1]).

APPLES, STICKS, AND STONES

But the fruit of the Spirit is . . . gentleness and self-control.

GALATIANS 5:22–23

A word fitly spoken
is like apples of gold in a setting of silver.

PROVERBS 25:11[2]

Words are such powerful things, Father.

When we're little, we say that "sticks and stones will break my bones, but words will never hurt me."

But words *do* hurt! They break hearts and homes, and sometimes we carry those hurts for years.

Yet words also do good! "A word fitly spoken" is a beautiful thing, "like apples of gold in a setting of silver" (Proverbs 25:11[2]).

You tell us that "the tongue has the power of life and death, and those who love it will eat its fruit" (18:21).

So today I pray that the words _____ speaks will bear good fruit, fruit that brings life and health to others.

Please give her wisdom with words, Lord. "Wise words satisfy like a good meal; the right words bring satisfaction" (v. 20[1]).

So may her words be satisfying because they are filled with your love and your Spirit.

May she have a way with words, Lord Jesus. *Your* way! May the fruit of your Spirit, your "gentleness and self-control" (Galatians 5:23), be evident in what she says and does.

Help her to watch her words closely. You told us that "on the day of judgment," we will "give account for every careless word" (Matthew 12:36–37[2]).

How we need your help in this! "We all make many mistakes" (James 3:2[1]). If we could learn to control our tongues, we "could also control ourselves in every other way."

How often we wish we could pull words back as soon as they come out of our mouths. Help her to be "quick to listen, slow to speak and slow to become angry" (1:19).

I ask that you will help _____ to choose her words carefully when emotions run hot, because "a gentle answer deflects anger, but harsh words make tempers flare" (Proverbs 15:1[1]).

Please also give her the wisdom to understand that gossip is a hurtful sin. "A troublemaker plants seeds of strife; gossip separates the best of friends" (16:28[1]). "The words of the wicked are like a murderous ambush, but the words of the godly save lives" (12:6[1]).

Be in her words, Jesus! I pray they will point to you with power and love.

May the words she uses "be good and helpful," and "encouragement to those who hear them" (Ephesians 4:29[1]).

May "the message" about you, "in all its richness," fill her life (Colossians 3:16[1])!

WEEK 8

THANKFUL

More Yours Than Mine

I would maintain that thanks are the highest form of thought,
and that gratitude is happiness doubled by wonder.

G. K. CHESTERTON

Her name meant "favored by God," but she didn't always feel that way.

Hannah had prayed and prayed for God to give her a child. One day she pleaded with God so passionately that when Eli the priest overheard her, "he thought she had been drinking" (1 Samuel 1:13[1]).

Not long afterward, Hannah's prayers were answered. She gave the baby a name that would perpetually remind her and others of how God had answered her prayer. She named him Samuel, which means "heard by God" (see v. 20).

But a name wasn't enough—Hannah was just getting started. When Samuel was a little older, she brought him back to Eli. "Sir, do you remember me?" Hannah asked. "I am the very woman who stood here several years ago praying to the LORD. I asked the LORD to give me this boy, and he has granted my request. Now I am giving him to the LORD, and he will belong to the LORD his whole life" (vv. 26–28[1]).

Samuel was a gift from God, and Hannah knew it. She was so thankful that she *gave him up* to God, doing her best to help Samuel know, love, and serve the Lord as long as he lived.

He would become one of the greatest prophets and leaders in Israel's history.

Hannah didn't just *say* "thank you" to God. She *lived* her thankfulness. An entire nation was blessed for generations as a result. And it all started with a passionate prayer.

God's best blessings come into our children's lives when we energetically pray for them. This week we're thanking God for our children as well as praying for thankfulness in their hearts. You'll find prayers about practical matters like attitudes, accepting our bodies the way God made them, strength and joy in the face of fear, enjoying God's creation, thoughtfulness for others, and more.

I hope you'll remember Hannah as you pray. She was so thankful for her child that she gave him to God every day. She realized that her child belonged to Him even more than he did to her, and she passionately prayed for God's will to be done in his life.

Shouldn't we do the same?

GRATITUDE ATTITUDE

Give thanks in all circumstances; for this is
God's will for you in Christ Jesus.

1 THESSALONIANS 5:18

The first time I saw her, I was so thankful, Father.

Ten tiny fingers. Ten perfect pink toes. A tender, priceless gift from your heart and hand.

I was grateful then, and I still am. How could I not be? How blessed I am to have a child!

I pray you will help us to be thankful even for little things, Lord. Isn't that one of the secrets to a happy life?

Everything starts with you. Every gift. Every moment. Every breath. You are "the Creator" and are "worthy of eternal praise" (Romans 1:25[1]).

So I praise you for life, Lord. And I praise you even more for the privilege of knowing you!

I pray that you will help me and my child to learn to "be thankful in all circumstances," because this is your "will" for us (1 Thessalonians 5:18[1]).

If she is able to keep her eyes on you, she'll always have something to be thankful for, even when life is hard.

Thank you for your example in this, Jesus. Even when you were wrongfully arrested, beaten, and crucified, you "gave thanks to God" (1 Corinthians 11:24[1]).

Your closeness to the Father and your ability to keep your eyes on what matters show us what our own hearts should be like.

Please help us to "press on to know" you (Hosea 6:3[1]), Jesus!

You gave yourself for us so that we "should no longer live" for ourselves but for you "who died for" us and were "raised again" (2 Corinthians 5:15).

I confess that our attitudes aren't always what they should be, Lord.

Please fill us with yourself so that fresh thankfulness overflows into every part of our lives. May it transform our attitudes about life and everything we expect from it.

Help us to make "every thought captive" to you (10:5[2]) so that each day we discover new opportunities to be grateful.

And when we find it hard to be thankful because of our circumstances, please help us to learn how to thank you by faith, so that we "continually offer" to you "a sacrifice of praise—the fruit of lips that openly profess" your name (Hebrews 13:15).

Yes, Lord! Help us to thank you in advance for the goodness that awaits us in you.

"Whatever" we do, "whether in word or deed," may we "do it all in" your name, loving you and "giving thanks to God the Father" through you (Colossians 3:17).

We can always be thankful for you!

HEART MUSIC

Sing and make music from your heart to the
Lord, always giving thanks to God the Father for
everything, in the name of our Lord Jesus Christ.

EPHESIANS 5:19–20

I love to hear my child sing, Lord.

It doesn't even matter if he hits the right notes—it's just good to hear his voice.

Something tells me that you feel the same way. You made us to sing, just as your Word teaches us.

"Sing praises to God, sing praises; sing praises to our King, sing praises" (Psalm 47:6)!

"Is anyone happy? Let them sing songs of praise" (James 5:13).

"Let all who take refuge in you be glad; let them ever sing for joy" (Psalm 5:11).

I pray that _____ will always want to "sing and make music" (Ephesians 5:19) in his heart to you, Jesus.

We sing when we're happy. May he be happy in you!

May he have the happiness that springs from a thankful soul, because he has a heartfelt relationship with you.

May he know he's a child of the King. Then he will "be grateful for receiving a kingdom that cannot be shaken" (Hebrews 12:28[2]) and worship you for it.

May he say from the heart, "I will sing the LORD's praise, for he has been good to me" (Psalm 13:6).

I ask also that your songs will fill his mind instead of the world's music. Sometimes songs get stuck in our heads, so I pray his thoughts will be stuck on you!

May he even sing "songs in the night" (77:6) because he lives without fear and knows that "even the darkness will not be dark to you," for "darkness is as light to you" (139:12).

I pray he will rest in you and "sing for joy in the shadow of your wings" (63:7[1]).

What could be better than knowing you will always watch over us?

"You guide" us "with your counsel, and afterward you will take" us "into glory" (73:24).

But until then, you build us up. We "go from strength to strength" (84:7) when we set our hearts on you.

May his life be a symphony of praise to you, Lord, a masterpiece of melodies from the heart—a joy for you to hear!

May he say, "I will sing to the LORD as long as I live. I will praise my God to my last breath!" (104:33[1]).

Then the music of his life will only grow sweeter. He'll join with "every creature in heaven and on earth and under the earth and on the sea," singing, "To him who sits on the throne and to the Lamb be praise and honor and glory and power, for ever and ever!" (Revelation 5:13).

OVER WHAT'S UNDER THE BED

> Let them praise his name with dancing
> and make music to him. . . .
> For the LORD takes delight in his people;
> he crowns the humble with victory.
> Let his faithful people rejoice in this honor
> and sing for joy on their beds.
>
> PSALM 149:3–5

Sometimes children want us to leave a night-light on, close the closet door, and check under the bed.

Nighttime isn't always easy. It's hard to sleep when imaginations run wild.

So I pray that you'll calm my child's heart with your peace. Please chase her fears away so she awakens to the bright new day of your love, where "joy comes in the morning" (Psalm 30:5[3]).

I ask that she'll not only rest in you; may she really "rejoice" in you (Philippians 3:1[2]), even if that means "dancing" and singing "for joy" (Psalm 149:3, 5) on her bed!

You told your people, "You will go free, leaping with joy like calves let out to pasture" (Malachi 4:2[1]).

May she know the joy David did: "The LORD is my strength and my shield; my heart trusts in him, and he helps me. My heart leaps for joy, and with my song I praise him" (Psalm 28:7).

There's no joy like the joy you give. May it be something she treasures all her life.

I also ask that it will be something she gives away. I pray that she'll let her "light shine before others, so that they may see" (Matthew 5:16[2]) the good things she does and praise you for them.

May she live for "the praise" of your "glory" (Ephesians 1:12), enthusiastic in your love, pointing others to you!

However many years she sees, I pray she'll always "receive the kingdom of God like a child" (Mark 10:15[2]), with a fresh, open-eyed faith that looks forward to each new day.

But I also ask that you bless her with a mature, "even-though" faith: "Even though the fig trees have no blossoms, and there are no grapes on the vines; even though the olive crop fails, and the fields lie empty and barren; even though the flocks die in the fields, and the cattle barns are empty, yet I will rejoice in the LORD! I will be joyful in the God of my salvation!" (Habakkuk 3:17–18[1]).

Please bless her with a faith that stays steady through the ups and downs of life, because you are over all of it.

May she always be thankful for you, Father. You promise in your Word, "My servants will sing out of the joy of their hearts" (Isaiah 65:14).

May her heart sing and dance in the joy of your presence today, tomorrow, and always.

VIRTUOUS REALITY

> O LORD, what a variety of things you have made!
> In wisdom you have made them all.
> The earth is full of your creatures. . . .
> May the glory of the LORD continue forever!
> The LORD takes pleasure in all he has made!
>
> PSALM 104:24, 31[1]

The beauty of what you've made takes my breath away.

The majesty of a midnight sky, the wonder of a baby's hand, the sunset you paint each day . . . So many masterpieces!

I can see why you "looked over all" you'd made and "saw that it was very good!" (Genesis 1:31[1]).

You spoke it into existence, and there it was . . . sun, moon and stars, worlds beyond counting.

I pray _____ will never lose a sense of wonder at all you've made. May she be enthralled by "the work of your hands" (Hebrews 1:10).

I pray she'll spend time outside enjoying what you've made, choosing your brilliance over the dull flicker of virtual reality.

"The heavens proclaim" your "glory," and "the skies display" your "craftsmanship" (Psalm 19:1[1]). "Day after day they continue to speak; night after night they make" you "known" (v. 2[1]).

As she takes in beauty around her, may she sense your creative genius and power.

"All things were made through" you (John 1:3²)! Science may help us understand *how* some things happen, but it doesn't tell us *why*. Speak to her spirit, Lord. Give her a glimpse of the love in your artistry.

We were "created for" your "glory," "formed and made" (Isaiah 43:7) so we may know and praise you with "all your works" (Psalm 145:10²).

Your Word tells us that "the creation looks forward to the day when it will join" your children "in glorious freedom from death and decay" (Romans 8:21¹). It says, "Let the rivers clap their hands; let the hills sing for joy together" (Psalm 98:8²). "Let the fields and their crops burst out with joy! Let the trees of the forest sing for joy" before you, for you are "coming!" (96:12–13¹).

You are coming to take all that's wrong and set it right. One day, you'll create "a new heaven and a new earth" (Revelation 21:1²).

If there's so much beauty in the world now, I can only imagine what it will be like then! Not a hint of sin or death . . . the virtuous reality you intended before the dawn of "the first day" (Genesis 1:5²).

I pray my child will "look forward" to the day of your return and "speed its coming," Lord Jesus (2 Peter 3:12), so she may live an undying life in the goodness of your presence forever.

COMPASSION'S REWARD

And if you give even a cup of cold water to one of the
least of my followers, you will surely be rewarded.

MATTHEW 10:42[1]

Your Word tells of so many times when you "had compassion" for others (Matthew 9:36[2]), Jesus.

When you "saw a large crowd" and then "healed their sick" (14:14).

When you encountered "two blind men" who "were sitting by the roadside" (20:30).

When "a man with leprosy" came to you and "begged" before you "on his knees" (Mark 1:40).

Each time you served and helped them.

You are "full of compassion and mercy" (James 5:11), so I pray that my child will "have the same attitude" (Philippians 2:5[1]).

Please give him a humble, compassionate heart like yours, Lord.

Help him not to "look out" only for his "own interests" (v. 4[1]). May he "take an interest in others, too."

May his compassion flow from a thankful heart because he's mindful of your "great love" and knows "the wonderful things" you have done for him (Psalm 107:15[1]).

You promised that he'll "be rewarded" for even the little things like giving "a cup of cold water" (Matthew 10:42[1]), so I ask that he will show kindness in ways large and small.

When he goes through struggles, please use those moments to help him feel deeply for others who wrestle in the same ways.

May he discover that you comfort us "in all our troubles, so that we can comfort those in any trouble with the comfort we ourselves receive" from you (2 Corinthians 1:4).

Your Word teaches that "pure and genuine religion in the sight of God the Father means caring for orphans and widows in their distress and refusing to let the world corrupt" us (James 1:27[1]).

Please keep him from the world's selfish ways, Lord, and help him to look after those who have less than he does.

Help him not to focus on what he doesn't have; help him instead to see all he does have just because he belongs to you.

I ask that he'll learn to "do good to everyone—especially to those in the family of faith" (Galatians 6:10[1]).

May your love grow "more perfect" in him as he lives "like" you "here in this world" (1 John 4:17[1]).

Because you served us so humbly, Jesus, the Father lifted you "to the place of highest honor" and gave you "the name above all other names" (Philippians 2:9[1]).

Then _____ will be rewarded too, because you are the "one thing" he seeks (Psalm 27:4) most of all!

RISE AND SHINE!

For we are God's masterpiece. He has created
us anew in Christ Jesus, so we can do the good
things he planned for us long ago.

EPHESIANS 2:10[1]

May _____ be thankful for the way you made her, Father.

You made her a "masterpiece" (Ephesians 2:10[1])!

You "formed" her in her "mother's womb" (Ecclesiastes 11:5), weaving each strand of DNA into a one-of-a-kind creation. There's never been anyone like her, and there never will be.

I pray she'll rest content in the truth that she doesn't need to be anyone other than the original you made her to be.

So many people spend their lives wanting to be someone else, chasing after others who are following their "pride" (Zephaniah 3:11[3]), living for the trends of this world.

May she follow you instead, and want to be what you made her to be!

You made her to know you and love you and "have life" through your Son (1 John 5:12[2]), a full life brimming with purpose.

You have such "good things" (Ephesians 2:10[1]) planned for her. I pray she'll embrace your ideas for life and live with anticipation, looking forward to each new day with you.

No one is as creative as you, Lord! "Who can know" your "thoughts" (Romans 11:34[1])? "Everything comes from" you "and exists by" your "power and is intended for" your "glory" (v. 36[1]).

Please give her grace to understand that there can be no beauty in this world apart from you. You are the source of all that "is good" (Psalm 85:12[2]).

When I think about when _____ was born, I was thrilled to see the wonder of your work. She was precious and beautiful, just the way you made her.

And the more she walks with you, the more beautiful she'll become, filled with "the radiance" of your light that shines from the inside when your Son lives in us (Hebrews 1:3).

"You are the fountain of life, the light by which we see!" (Psalm 36:9[1]).

I pray she'll "arise" each day with the fresh new life you give and "shine for all to see" as "the glory" of who you are "rises to shine" (Isaiah 60:1[1]) on her soul. May she shine for you!

May she display your "glory" (2 Corinthians 3:18[4]) and your beauty as you "work out" your "plans" for her "life" (Psalm 138:8[1]).

May she rise to praise you each new day, thankful that through "Jesus there is forgiveness" for sins (Acts 13:38[1]).

I ask that she may "know the greatness" of all that you are (Psalm 135:5[1]) and live for nothing less than to love you for all eternity.

DO IT AGAIN!

LORD, I have heard of your fame;
I stand in awe of your deeds, LORD.
Repeat them in our day,
in our time make them known.

HABAKKUK 3:2

I'm amazed when I think about the things you've done, Lord.

You fed "five thousand men" and even more "women and children" (Matthew 14:21[2]) with "only five loaves of bread and two fish" (v. 17).

You walked "on the water" (John 6:19) and calmed "the wind and the sea" (Mark 4:41[2]) just by speaking to them.

You made "the blind see" and "the lame walk" (Matthew 11:5[1]). You cured "those with leprosy" and made "the deaf hear." You even raised "the dead" to "life"!

And you continue to "stretch out your hand to heal and perform signs and wonders" through your powerful "name" (Acts 4:30).

I praise you for all you do, and I pray _____ will see your hand move too! I long for him to see "your works and meditate on all your mighty deeds" (Psalm 77:12).

"I stand in awe of your deeds," and ask that you "repeat them" in his day and "make them known" in his time (Habakkuk 3:2).

"Summon your power, God," and "show us your strength . . . as you have done before" (Psalm 68:28).

May he see your hand move because he has faith in you.

There was a place where you "did not do many miracles" because of "their lack of faith" (Matthew 13:58). Don't let him live there, Lord!

Let him have a deep and lasting faith in you so that he sees what you can do.

I also ask that his faith won't depend on miracles alone; then he would "never believe" in you unless he sees "miraculous signs and wonders" (John 4:48[1]).

Please build my faith too, Jesus. "I do believe; help me overcome my unbelief!" (Mark 9:24).

May I set "an example" for him "in conduct, in love, in faith, in purity" (1 Timothy 4:12[2]), so that we both may "become like little children" in our faith (Matthew 18:3).

Little children say "Do it again!" when grown-ups do something they love. I think about what you've done and I pray, "Do it again!"

"I stand in awe of your deeds, LORD. Repeat them in our day!" (Habakkuk 3:2).

I long for him to have faith that surpasses my own so that he will see you do even more.

You "alone" do "great wonders," Lord, and your faithful "love endures forever" (Psalm 136:4).

I thank you for the ways you've shown yourself faithful in my life—and I praise you in advance for what my child will see when you do it again!

WEEK 9

HUMBLE

Me Third

We must view humility as one of the essential
things that characterizes true Christianity.

JONATHAN EDWARDS

If we want our children to really know and be like Jesus,
we'll pray for them to be humble.

When we think of must-have character traits for our children, humility may not be one of the first things that come to mind. But it should be if we really want them to be blessed.

God loves to bless humble people. The Bible emphasizes this again and again. "God opposes the proud but shows favor to the humble" (1 Peter 5:5). "He guides the humble in what is right and teaches them his way" (Psalm 25:9), and "crowns the humble with victory" (149:4).

While God's Word tells us to be "completely humble" (Ephesians 4:2), that isn't the world's way. Living with humility requires a special kind of strength in our me-first world.

It takes strength to admit when you're wrong, to say that you're sorry, or to share the credit when you've done most of the work. When the world tells us to "be somebody," God says we will be happier if we take our eyes off ourselves and work on serving Him and others. Being humble comes with a price to our pride, but it also comes with a promise: "Humble yourselves before the Lord, and he will lift you up" (James 4:10).

If we want our children to know the real height and depth of God's love, we'll ask God to help them have humble hearts. Jesus was "gentle and humble in heart" and promised that if we "learn" from Him, we will "find rest" for our "souls" (Matthew 11:29). He set "an example" (John 13:15) for us and can be trusted to deliver on what He promises.

> Though he was God,
>   he did not think of equality with God
>   as something to cling to.
> Instead, he gave up his divine privileges. . . .
>
> Therefore, God elevated him to the place of
>   highest honor
> and gave him the name above all other names.
>   (Philippians 2:6–7, 9[1])

Asking God to help our children be humble challenges us to be humble ourselves. We have to trust God with our most prized possessions. Praying this way isn't always easy, but as Ruth Bell Graham pointed out, "The Christian parent's authority will be a direct result of, and in proportion to, his or her submission to divine authority."[9] If we want to make a vital and lasting impact on our children, we'll ask for what matters most to God.

An old Puritan prayer pleads,

Let me learn by paradox
    that the way down is the way up,
    that to be low is to be high,
    that the broken heart is the healed heart,
    that the contrite spirit is the rejoicing spirit,
    that the repenting soul is the victorious soul,
    that to have nothing is to possess all,
    that to bear the cross is to wear the crown,
    that to give is to receive.[10]

The prayers in the pages to come are intended to point our children to the "narrow gate" (Matthew 7:13) of Jesus's humility.

From the first moment we lay eyes on our children, we would give them anything. But God can give them even more. "God blesses those who are humble, for they will inherit the whole earth" (5:5[1]).

LIFE BEYOND LABELS

Should you then seek great things for
yourself? Do not seek them.

JEREMIAH 45:5

Most parents dream that their children will do great things,
don't they, Jesus?

We like to look at their achievements and pray they'll go far.

But there can be a lot in a look, and pride can get the better
of us. Your Word says that "haughty eyes, a proud heart,
and evil actions are all sin" (Proverbs 21:4[1]).

So I ask that you help me to want what you want as I dream
of what my child might be.

Whoever follows you "will never walk in darkness, but will
have the light of life" (John 8:12). My son needs your "light
to shine" (12:46[1]) on him to direct his steps.

Instead of seeking great things for himself, help him to follow
you. You tell us, "Don't be impressed with your own wisdom"
(Proverbs 3:7[1]). "The wisdom of this world is foolishness"
to you (1 Corinthians 3:19[3]).

Keep him free from the "love of money" and help him to
"be content" with what he has (Hebrews 13:5), because
"the love of money is the root of all kinds of evil. And some
people, craving money, have wandered from the true faith and
pierced themselves with many sorrows" (1 Timothy 6:10[1]).

But if he seeks your kingdom "above all else" and lives "righteously," he will have everything he needs (Matthew 6:33[1]).

Give him wisdom to see through "hollow and deceptive" thinking "which depends on human tradition" and the principles "of this world" instead of you (Colossians 2:8).

Help him to see beyond labels and titles, Lord. May his heart be devoted to you.

Teach him "to realize the brevity of life" (Psalm 90:12[1]). "Like the morning fog—it's here a little while, then it's gone" (James 4:14[1]).

But eternity awaits. May he be ready!

Protect his soul as he studies and learns. Give him teachers who know you and love you.

You oppose "the proud" but give grace "to the humble" (1 Peter 5:5[2]). Help him to live in your strength and not his own. Then he'll really accomplish something!

"How great is the goodness you have stored up for those who fear you. You lavish it on those who come to you for protection, blessing them before the watching world. You hide them in the shelter of your presence" (Psalm 31:19–20[1]).

I pray that your favor may rest on him so he may use every gift you've given him and be blessed in all he does.

"Establish the work" of his hands, Lord (90:17[2]), so that all he does is for you!

BROKEN
AND BLESSED

I tell you, her sins—and they are many—have been
forgiven, so she has shown me much love. But a
person who is forgiven little shows only little love.

LUKE 7:47[1]

Your forgiveness is so beautiful, Jesus.

It cost you everything. But all we have to do is ask, and you
"remove our" sins from us "as far as the east is from the
west" (Psalm 103:12[2]).

You even tell us you'll remember our sins "no more" (Isaiah
43:25)!

No wonder the woman whose many sins you forgave "loved
much" (Luke 7:47[2]). How could she not?

But rich as your "kindness and restraint and patience" are
(Romans 2:4[5]), the human heart "is deceitful above all things
and desperately wicked" (Jeremiah 17:9[3]).

How easy it is for our hearts to be "hardened by the deceitfulness of sin" (Hebrews 3:13[2])!

What starts as just a "small" sin in our eyes—one little
compromise—can take us to dark places where we never
thought we'd go.

So today I pray for my daughter's heart, Jesus. May her heart
be soft and sensitive to you.

You say in your Word, "I will give you a new heart, and I will put a new spirit in you. I will take out your stony, stubborn heart and give you a tender, responsive heart. And I will put my Spirit in you so that you will follow" (Ezekiel 36:26–27[1]).

I pray she will be free to "walk in your ways" (2 Chronicles 6:31[2]) and will love you generously.

Protect her from sin's deceitfulness, so that her mind won't become "dark and confused" (Romans 1:21[1]). May she see that your "kindness is intended to lead" us to repentance (2:4).

May she "be transformed by the renewing" of her mind (12:2[3]), with her thinking inspired by the genius of your Spirit instead of our culture's catwalk of conformity that dresses us in chains.

Help her to stay close to you so she'll know the gentle promptings of your Spirit. May she daily discern you saying, "This is the way, walk in it" (Isaiah 30:21[2]).

Please let her understand how sin hurts your heart so she may not "grieve the Holy Spirit" (Ephesians 4:30[2]). May she love you so much that she wants to stay away from sin.

Jesus, the woman who showed you "much love" (Luke 7:47[1]) may have been broken, but she was also blessed! You told her, "Your faith has saved you; go in peace" (v. 50).

I pray my daughter will also bow before you with a humble and loving faith, so that she may be set free to walk into life in the beauty of your peace.

HEALTHY FEAR

Come, my children, listen to me;
I will teach you the fear of the LORD.

PSALM 34:11

I've tried to teach him to have healthy fear, Father. You've seen each moment . . .

"Look both ways before you cross the street." "Don't pet a dog if he's growling." "Stay out of the deep end until you can swim."

Some lessons stuck. Some he learned the hard way.

Please give him wisdom that keeps him from harm and blesses him. Help him to have respect and reverence for you.

Your Word says, "The fear of the LORD is the beginning of wisdom" (Psalm 111:10[2]). You even promise to "bless those who fear" you (115:13)!

So I pray _____ will both adore you and have a healthy respect for all you are. You are "glorious in holiness, awesome in splendor" (Exodus 15:11[1]).

"O LORD, what are human beings that you should notice them, mere mortals that you should think about them?" (Psalm 144:3[1]).

But you do! In such tender ways—"even the hairs" of our heads "are all numbered" (Matthew 10:30[2]).

So please help him to have respect that leads to love. When he understands that you're both powerful and loving, he'll know you are "mighty to save" (Isaiah 63:1).

Nothing can stop you, and no one is stronger than you! May you be his "sure foundation," blessing him with "salvation and wisdom and knowledge" (33:6). Living with reverence for all you are is "the key to this treasure."

May he "work hard to show the results" of his salvation, "obeying" you "with deep reverence" (Philippians 2:12[1]). Not out of "fear of punishment"—because then he would not have "fully experienced" your "perfect love" (1 John 4:18[1]).

May he learn to "trust in" you "with all" his heart, instead of depending on his "own understanding" (Proverbs 3:5[2]).

Your Word promises that "the fear of the LORD leads to life, and whoever has it rests satisfied" (19:23[2]). Thank you, Father, that when we come to you, we do not come "to a place of flaming fire, darkness, gloom, and whirlwind, as the Israelites did at Mount Sinai" (Hebrews 12:18[1]).

Through your Son's kindness to us, we "have come to Mount Zion, to the city of the living God, the heavenly Jerusalem" (v. 22). We "have come to thousands upon thousands of angels in joyful assembly."

Oh, to be part of that! To join all of heaven praising you together, saying, "Holy, holy, holy, is the Lord God Almighty, who was and is and is to come!" (Revelation 4:8[2]).

CONSTRUCTIVE CRITICISM

If you listen to constructive criticism,
you will be at home among the wise.
If you reject discipline, you only harm yourself.

PROVERBS 15:31–32[1]

I pray that _____ will learn to accept "constructive criticism," Father (Proverbs 15:31[1]).

He'll need to "listen to advice and accept instruction" (19:20[2]) if he's going to do well.

So I ask that he'll be able to "accept correction" (Zephaniah 3:7[2]) with grace that flows out of a heart that is secure in you.

If he takes to heart that you love and accept him unconditionally, his learning and growing will be easier.

But listening to constructive criticism isn't easy! It takes humility, wisdom, maturity, and faith.

May he be humble enough to intently "listen to correction" (Proverbs 15:32[1]), understanding that "with humility comes wisdom" (11:2).

Give him wisdom to "test" whether what he hears is genuinely from you (1 John 4:1[2]), or if it is simply offered in a critical spirit not intended to help. Guide him so that he can "reject the wrong and choose the right" (Isaiah 7:15).

When he has willfully "strayed from your path" (Psalm 44:18), help him to have the strength to "repent" and "turn away from" all his "offenses" (Ezekiel 18:30). Your Word says that "a rebuke impresses a discerning person" (Proverbs 17:10). May he be one!

I know you'll encourage him as he walks with you, Jesus. May he be "mature and fully assured" (Colossians 4:12[2]) so that he's strong enough to learn from his mistakes.

Your Word teaches us that if you "reprove a wise man," they "will love you" (Proverbs 9:8[2]). Give him that kind of heart!

May he have the ability to step back and look at himself without being defensive, so that he can realize where he needs to improve.

When the learning curve is steep and life is hard, I pray he'll persevere and stay close, because you lead "the humble in doing right" (Psalm 25:9[1]).

When you seem distant and he cannot see your hand at work, help him to trust in your love, because you are "the faithful one" (Isaiah 49:7[1]).

Please give him a desire for excellence so that he will be "truly competent" in his life and work (Proverbs 22:29[1]). You created him to love you in everything he does; may he serve and represent you well!

I praise you that you "will work out" your "plans" for his life—"for your faithful love, O LORD, endures forever" (Psalm 138:8[1])!

THIRD PLACE WINS!

You know that the rulers in this world lord it over their
people, and officials flaunt their authority over those under
them. But among you it will be different. Whoever wants to be
a leader among you must be your servant, and whoever wants
to be first among you must be the slave of everyone else. For
even the Son of Man came not to be served but to serve others.

MARK 10:42–45[1]

Jesus, you "came not to be served but to serve others" and
to give your life "as a ransom for many" (Mark 10:45[1]).

Even though you "and the father are one" (John 10:30[2]), you
"did not think of equality with God as something to cling
to" (Philippians 2:6[1]). Instead, you "gave up" your "divine
privileges" (v. 7[1]). You "took the humble position of a slave"
and were "born as a human being."

You even "died a criminal's death on a cross" (v. 8[1])!

Your humility is awe-inspiring, and I worship you for it.

You didn't have to do it, but you did it out of love.

I pray my child will be so much like you that he'll serve
others as well.

Your Word tells how you were "moved with compassion"
(Mark 1:41[5]). I pray that _____ may also be moved by
others' needs.

May he see the beauty of putting himself *third*—you first,
others second, then himself.

I ask that he'll feel a special closeness to you as he looks to others' needs, understanding that he's somehow caring for you at the same time. Isn't that how you described it, Jesus? You said, "Whatever you did for one of the least of these . . . , you did for me" (Matthew 25:40).

You said that third place wins . . . that "the last will be first, and the first last" (20:16²)!

As I pray that _____ will love third place, I ask this for myself as well.

It's not the world's way, but it's your way. You promise that others "will know that" we belong to you if we genuinely "love one another" (John 13:35).

There's no limit to your love! How "great is your love, higher than the heavens; your faithfulness reaches to the skies" (Psalm 108:4).

You "live in a high and holy place" but also with those who are "contrite and lowly in spirit" (Isaiah 57:15). The scope of your love is breathtaking, and I praise you for it!

Please help us to "humble" ourselves before you, so that you "will lift" us up (James 4:10).

BLESSED BY DISCIPLINE

My child, don't reject the LORD's discipline,
and don't be upset when he corrects you.
For the LORD corrects those he loves,
just as a father corrects a child in whom he delights.

PROVERBS 3:11–12[1]

I pray for _____ in those moments when you'll have to discipline him, Father.

Your discipline is never easy. "No discipline seems pleasant at the time, but painful" (Hebrews 12:11). But afterward "it produces a harvest of righteousness and peace for those who have been trained by it."

Every time you disciplined me, you were right to do it. When I willfully strayed from your path, you corrected me and showed me "the consequences" of my actions (Ezekiel 44:10). Yet you didn't do it in anger but in love, just as a "father corrects a child in whom he delights" (Proverbs 3:12[1]).

But it was tough! Sometimes I *felt* like you were angry. I'm reminded of David's prayer: "LORD, do not rebuke me in your anger or discipline me in your wrath. . . . My soul is in deep anguish. How long, LORD, how long? Turn, LORD, and deliver me; save me because of your unfailing love" (Psalm 6:1, 3–4).

There were times when you felt so far away and others when "your hand of discipline was heavy on me" and "my strength evaporated like water" (32:4[1]).

"When you hid your face, I was dismayed" (30:7), but then "I acknowledged my sin to you," and "you forgave" me (32:5).

I know there are times when _____ will need to confess his sins and ask for forgiveness also, Jesus.

You are "the one who is truly righteous" and "the sacrifice that atones for our sins" (1 John 2:1–2[1]), and I praise you for it!

Your Word tells us "everyone undergoes discipline" (Hebrews 12:8). If we do not, we "are not really" your "children at all" (v. 8[1]). So I pray that he'll not "make light" of your "discipline" or "give up" when you correct him (v. 5[1]).

May he have a humble, tender heart and confess his sin with "godly sorrow" that "brings repentance" (2 Corinthians 7:10).

Abba, your discipline is perfect. You discipline "the one" you love (Hebrews 12:6[2]), and we are blessed as a result.

Your discipline "is always good for us, so that we might share in" your "holiness" (v. 10[1]). "Joyful are those you discipline, LORD, those you teach with your instructions" (Psalm 94:12[1]).

So may he "submit" to you, "the Father of spirits," and "live" (Hebrews 12:9)!

"I DID IT"

If we confess our sins, he is faithful and just and will forgive
us our sins and purify us from all unrighteousness.

1 JOHN 1:9

I pray that _____ will have the humility to admit when
she is wrong, Father. Sometimes that's so hard for us to do!

I think of Adam shifting blame. When you asked him about
the forbidden fruit, he told you, "The woman you put here
with me—she gave me some fruit from the tree, and I ate
it" (Genesis 3:12).

And Eve did the same thing. She told you, "The serpent
deceived me, and I ate" (v. 13).

How many times have I also blamed others even when I knew
in my heart I was wrong?

Thank you that you want to teach us another way, "your
way" (Psalm 27:11²). How we need you to "show" us "your
ways" (25:4), Father!

You tell us, "My thoughts are not your thoughts, neither are
your ways my ways" (Isaiah 55:8²).

So I ask that my daughter accept responsibility for her actions.

May she understand that admitting sins and faults doesn't
make her less of a person—it makes her more of one in your
eyes. Your Word tells us that "humility comes before honor"
(Proverbs 15:33²), and that you "beautify the humble with
salvation" (Psalm 149:4³).

May the beauty of your Spirit rest on her so that she walks before you with "integrity of heart and uprightness" (1 Kings 9:4[2]).

"I know, my God, that you examine our hearts and rejoice when you find integrity there" (1 Chronicles 29:17[1]). May she bring you joy!

May her integrity be rooted in her relationship with you, not in self-righteousness, because "no one living is righteous before you" (Psalm 143:2).

"It is through the grace of our Lord Jesus that we are saved" (Acts 15:11), and "if anyone thinks he is something, when he is nothing, he deceives himself" (Galatians 6:3[2]).

Even though admitting she is wrong may cost her in the world's eyes, only your eyes matter, and you see our "every step" (Job 34:21).

You're able to care for every need no matter what happens. You "make the righteous secure" (Psalm 7:9).

So I pray her "soul finds rest" in you, because her "salvation comes from" you (62:1).

Resting in you, she'll be truly secure—even secure enough to admit her faults! You tell us that "people who conceal their sins will not prosper, but if they confess and turn from them, they will receive mercy" (Proverbs 28:13[1]).

May she live in your mercy, Lord—and always love you for it!

PURE

"Tag, You're It!"

Blessed are the pure in heart, for they will see God.

MATTHEW 5:8

Innocence is God's gift. The wide eyes and open hearts of childhood remind us that we were created by someone who "is righteous in everything he does" and "is filled with kindness" (Psalm 145:17[1]).

But how we change with time. Hands close and hearts along with them—even to the point of shaking our fists at the sky. Once innocence is lost, can we ever get it back again?

Jesus answers that question in an unexpected place—the middle of a graveyard, where "day and night" a man wanders naked among the tombs, "howling and cutting himself with sharp stones" (Mark 5:5[1]).

He was once a mother's baby, but that was years before. Now he was the one his family mentioned only in whispers (if they spoke of him at all). We don't know his name. When

Jesus asked for it, the man answered, "My name is Legion, . . . for we are many" (v. 9).

But that wasn't his real name, and Jesus knew it. And by the time He finished with him, the man was "sitting there" at Jesus's feet, "fully clothed and perfectly sane" (v. 15[1]).

You might think the story ends there, but it's really only beginning. Jesus didn't just set the man free from a "legion of demons" (v. 15). The man "begged to go with" Jesus (v. 18), but the Lord instead sent him on a mission—even before He "began sending" the disciples (6:7[1]). Jesus told him, "Go home to your own people and tell them how much the Lord has done for you, and how he has had mercy on you" (5:19).

The man did what Jesus said . . . and more. Mark tells us that "the man started off to visit the Ten Towns of that region and began to proclaim the great things Jesus had done for him; and everyone was amazed at what he told them" (v. 20[1]).

You can only imagine those conversations. People used to cross the street when they saw him coming. But now, instead of gnashing his teeth at others, he smiles and says, "No, it's all right. Please come back. I have some really good news to share with you!"

His words had an impact. The next time Jesus visited this predominantly non-Jewish area, the people no longer pleaded with him "to go away and leave them alone" (v. 17[1]) as they had before. Instead, they "brought to him a man who was deaf and could hardly talk" (7:32). Then a crowd of "about 4,000" people gathered (8:9[1]).

So there you have it. A wasted, howling wreck of a man once known as "Legion" was transformed into one of history's first missionaries—and a highly effective one. All because "he ran" to Jesus (5:6), who is innocence found.

I wonder what effect his actions had on others over time. His story makes me think of one we used to tell as kids about a horrible monster that would chase you until you had nowhere else to run. Then he would reach out his scarred, scary hand and say . . . "Tag, you're it!"

Jesus touched the man's life, that man touched others, and they in turn reached out to others, and . . . who knows? Maybe twenty centuries later, one of them touched you and me.

Now it's our turn to "tag" our kids and point them back to Jesus. This week we're praying our children will discover the innocence only He can give. When we run to Jesus, He can forgive "our sins and purify us from all unrighteousness" (1 John 1:9). He can clean us up from the muck of the world so that we're "pure in heart" (Matthew 5:8), discovering life with fresh purpose. This week we'll pray that our children will "keep" themselves "in God's love" as they "wait for the mercy of our Lord Jesus Christ" to bring them "to eternal life" (Jude 1:21), and that they'll live in such a way that they may be deeply blessed.

These are prayers to address the effects of what has been called the "unholy trinity" of "the world, the flesh and the devil"[11] on our children. Nothing can stand against our Savior's love. Greater is He who is in us than he "who is in the world" (1 John 4:4).

DAY 64

CATCH HER DRIFT

Don't let me drift toward evil.
PSALM 141:4[1]

It can happen so easily, Father.

The world turns on its way, and we go along with it unaware.

Like a swimmer in a current who finds herself farther from shore than she ever meant to be, how easily we can "drift toward evil" (Psalm 141:4[1]), away from you.

Catch her drift, Lord. Don't let her be swept up in the world's ways, because "this world as we know it will soon pass away" (1 Corinthians 7:31[1]).

But "anyone who listens" to your teaching and follows it "is wise, like a person who builds a house on solid rock. Though the rain comes in torrents and the floodwaters rise and the winds beat against that house, it won't collapse because it is built on bedrock" (Matthew 7:24–25[1]).

I praise you, Jesus, that you save us from destruction as we turn to you. Because of your "great love we are not consumed"; your "compassions never fail" (Lamentations 3:22).

May her life be built on all you are! May her values come from your Word, not from media or the ever-shifting sands of the culture around us. Make her holy "by Your truth," Father (John 17:17[3]). "Your word is truth."

Help her to discern right and wrong through the gentle prompting of your Spirit.

Thank you that you have "sent the Spirit" of your Son "into our hearts, prompting us to call out, 'Abba, Father!'" (Galatians 4:6[1]).

Abba, "My prayer is not that you take" her "out of the world but that you protect" her "from the evil one" (John 17:15).

Strengthen her by your Spirit in her "inner being" (Ephesians 3:16[2]) so that she'll have wisdom to "keep away from worldly desires which wage war" against her very soul (1 Peter 2:11[1]).

Keep her from the pain and emptiness that result when we're "dragged away" by our "own evil desire and enticed" (James 1:14).

May she be "filled with love that comes from a pure heart, a clear conscience, and genuine faith" (1 Timothy 1:5[1]).

Give her grace to "run from anything that stimulates youthful lusts," and help her to instead "pursue righteous living, faithfulness, love, and peace" (2 Timothy 2:22[1]). Please give her close believing friends so that she may "enjoy the companionship of those who call on" you "with pure hearts."

May they look forward to you together, each day "encouraging one another" (Hebrews 10:25) in you, who are always worthy to receive "honor and glory and praise!" (Revelation 5:12).

WASH YOUR HANDS!

Come close to God, and God will come close to you.
Wash your hands, you sinners; purify your hearts, for
your loyalty is divided between God and the world.

JAMES 4:8[1]

Father, when I think about how holy you are, I'm reminded of what Isaiah said: "I am a man of unclean lips, and I live among a people of unclean lips" (Isaiah 6:5).

If you didn't save me, I would be completely "lost" (v. 5[2]).

But you have saved me. You saved me "not because of righteous things" I had done, "but because of" your "mercy" (Titus 3:5).

I praise you for "such a great salvation" (Hebrews 2:3[2])!

The only reason we love you is that you loved us "first" (1 John 4:19[3]). That makes me want to love you more! And when I draw closer to you, you come closer to me.

I pray that _____ will deeply desire to be close to you, and that your Spirit move in his heart "for this very purpose" (2 Corinthians 5:5).

I taught him how to wash his hands, but only you can wash his heart.

Only you can clean us up from our sins; you know how deeply stained we are. Even "our righteous acts are like filthy rags" before you (Isaiah 64:6).

"Who can say, 'I have kept my heart pure; I am clean and without sin'?" (Proverbs 20:9).

Yet you never give up on us! After you save us, your Spirit continues to change us, helping us grow and showing us where our "loyalty is divided" between you "and the world" (James 4:8[1]).

You keep on scrubbing! You gently tell us, "Come now, let us reason together, . . . though your sins are like scarlet, they shall be as white as snow" (Isaiah 1:18[2]).

You love us with "an everlasting love" that goes soul deep, drawing us near with an "unfailing kindness" (Jeremiah 31:3).

Oh, Father! May my son cherish your invincible, uncontainable love, and "honor" you "as holy" in his heart (Numbers 20:12).

May he have a heart sensitive to sin, so that he loves what you love. May your love make him bold—bold enough to know he can leave old sins behind and genuinely change, walking into innocence with you.

May he be quick to "seek reconciliation" with you and with others (Proverbs 14:9[1]).

I pray he will always understand that "we do not make requests of you because we are righteous, but because of your great mercy" (Daniel 9:18).

May the cry of his heart be, "Wash me," Lord, "and I shall be clean" (Psalm 51:7[2]).

Then with "clean hands and a pure heart" (24:4[2]), he'll know your joy forever!

FOR FRIENDS

Whoever walks with the wise becomes wise,
but the companion of fools will suffer harm.

PROVERBS 13:20[2]

Father, I ask for friends who will have a positive impact on
_____'s life.

I pray for believing friends so they may "encourage one another daily" (Hebrews 3:13).

Let them "build each other up" (1 Thessalonians 5:11) so they may live strong, effective lives for you.

I think about how Paul described Timothy: "I have no one else like him, who will show genuine concern" for others, not for his own purposes but for "those of Jesus Christ" (Philippians 2:20–21).

I want a friend like that for my daughter, Jesus!

Give her friends who have contagious, winsome faith, so they may "motivate one another to acts of love and good works" (Hebrews 10:24[1]).

Your Word says that "a friend loves at all times" (Proverbs 17:17[2]). May she have friends who love her unconditionally, celebrate her strengths, and patiently bear with her faults.

I pray for friends who will speak "the truth in love" (Ephesians 4:15[2]) and help her reach for her best, because "as iron sharpens iron, so a friend sharpens a friend" (Proverbs 27:17[1]).

"Faithful are the wounds of a friend" (v. 6[2]) who loves enough to tell the truth—even when it hurts.

Please also keep her from the hurt and harm foolish friends can cause; may she "walk with the wise and become wise" (13:20[1])!

Protect her from friends who would give no thought to you, who think "only about having a good time" (Ecclesiastes 7:4[1]). "Bad company corrupts good character" (1 Corinthians 15:33).

Please also keep her from those who seem to be wise but do not honor you "as God or give thanks" to you, who are "futile in their thinking" (Romans 1:21[2]) that human knowledge reigns supreme. "The world" does not know you "through its wisdom" (1 Corinthians 1:21).

But she can know you through your kindness! When you "our Savior revealed" your "kindness and love," you "saved us, not because of the righteous things we had done," but because of your "mercy" (Titus 3:4–5[1]). You "washed away our sins, giving us a new birth and new life through the Holy Spirit."

May your Spirit give life to her friendships, Lord!

You know how to make friendship work better than anyone else. "Greater love has no one than this, that someone lay down his life for his friends" (John 15:13[2]).

She could never have a better friend than you.

A SHINING STAR

Do everything without grumbling or arguing, so that
you may become blameless and pure, "children of God
without fault in a warped and crooked generation."
Then you will shine among them like stars in the
sky as you hold firmly to the word of life.

PHILIPPIANS 2:14–16

So many people want their kids to be stars, Lord. I see it everywhere . . . in pageants and programs and athletic events.

And I have to admit that sometimes I want the same thing. But I ask for something more: I pray that my son will shine for you.

May you, "the morning star," rise in his heart (2 Peter 1:19[2]).

Jesus, please keep him "from being polluted by the world" (James 1:27). Help him to "stay pure" by "obeying your word" (Psalm 119:9[1]).

May he be so in love with you that you fill his mind and heart. May he fix his "thoughts on what is true, and honorable, and right, and pure, and lovely, and admirable" (Philippians 4:8[1]). Lord, you are all of those things!

Let your love be so evident in him that it shows up on his face and radiates from within. May he have joy because of what you've done for him and live enthusiastically for you, "without grumbling or arguing" (2:14).

May his love for you exude from "a pure heart and a good conscience and a sincere faith" (1 Timothy 1:5[2]).

I pray that you'll empower him to "hold firmly to the word of life" (Philippians 2:16) so that others are drawn to you. Your Word tells us that "those who lead many to righteousness will shine like the stars forever" (Daniel 12:3[1]).

Let him shine, Lord! May he know the joy of seeing others come to you, Jesus.

Let him be there in that moment when dawn breaks and you, "the bright morning star" (Revelation 22:16[2]), shine with power in a life where darkness once reigned.

Let him see the miracle you can do in a soul, and praise you for it!

"Send out your light and your truth; let them lead" him (Psalm 43:3[2]).

Your "light shines on the godly, and joy on those whose hearts are right" (97:11[1]). May his heart be right with you!

I pray for "faith" that "is flourishing" and "love" that "is growing" (2 Thessalonians 1:3[1]) day by day.

You do "great things too marvelous to understand" (Job 9:10[1]). Every day you perform "countless miracles"!

I pray my son will know the joy of seeing you move in his life and the lives of others, and so take in with breathless wonder the beauty of heaven touching earth.

DESIRES

Take delight in the LORD,
and he will give you your heart's desires.
Commit everything you do to the LORD.
Trust him, and he will help you.

PSALM 37:4–5[1]

What you do with our desires is beautiful, Lord.

When we "take delight in" you, you give us our hearts' "desires" (Psalm 37:4[1]).

It's not that you give us whatever we want. You give us new and right desires . . . and then you fulfill them.

Only you give us lasting satisfaction! We were made for you. You know better than anyone what will make us happy.

So today I pray for _____'s desires and ask that you work in them.

Please help her to "discern what is pleasing" to you (Ephesians 5:10[2]), and to make that her goal for life.

"Every good and perfect gift" is from you; you do not change like the "shifting shadows" (James 1:17) of this world. You give what is original and best! Please help her not to be tripped up by the devil's counterfeits.

I pray she "will learn to know" your "will" for her, because it is "good and pleasing and perfect" (Romans 12:2[1]).

Help her to "put to death" the things that belong to her "earthly nature: sexual immorality, impurity, lust, evil desires and greed, which is idolatry. Because of these," your wrath "is coming" (Colossians 3:5–6).

Give her discernment to understand how important it is to walk closely with you so that she might "cling to" her "faith in Christ" and keep her "conscience clear" (1 Timothy 1:19[1]).

You will win her battles! You "fulfill the desire of those who fear" you; you "hear their cry and save them" (Psalm 145:19[3]).

Help her not to compartmentalize her life, just giving you part of it. May she "clothe" herself with your "presence," Lord Jesus, and not "think about ways to indulge" sinful desires (Romans 13:14[1]).

When that means tough choices, may she do what's right—instead of enjoying "the passing pleasures of sin" (Hebrews 11:25[3]).

You help us leave old sins behind us, because "through the power of the Spirit" we can "put to death the deeds" of our "sinful nature" (Romans 8:13[1]).

May "the Spirit renew" her "thoughts and attitudes," so she can "put on" her "new nature, created to be like" you—"truly righteous and holy" (Ephesians 4:23–24[1]).

"The mind governed by the Spirit is life and peace" (Romans 8:6). May she live with her heart at peace with you!

You satisfy our "desires with good things" (Psalm 103:5). May she discover the happiness you alone can give.

CROUCHING SIN AND SINGING ANGELS

Sin is crouching at your door; it desires to
have you, but you must rule over it.

GENESIS 4:7

There it is, lurking in the shadows . . . the same old sin that tripped her up before.

She knows better. But she does it anyway.

I'm afraid the forbidden fruit doesn't fall far from the family tree. "Everyone has sinned; we all fall short" of your "glorious standard" (Romans 3:23[1]).

I think of the number of times I've been stuck in a rut with a sin and the time it's taken to grow beyond it.

But you were "patient" with me and never gave up, always wanting me "to come to repentance" (2 Peter 3:9).

I praise you, Father, because even when "we are not faithful," you "remain faithful" (2 Timothy 2:13[4]).

"May I never boast about anything except" your cross, Jesus (Galatians 6:14[1])!

I love you, Holy Spirit, because even though my actions grieved you, you continued to "teach" me and "remind" me of my Savior's love (John 14:26).

So today I ask you to bless my daughter with the joy that comes from repenting.

Jesus, you said that "there is joy in the presence of God's angels when even one sinner repents" (Luke 15:10[1]). Wherever there is sin in her life, I pray she may have a change of heart that makes angels sing.

May your light that "produces only what is good and right and true" (Ephesians 5:9[1]) shine into her to dispel the darkness, transforming the way she thinks about things.

Please help her to understand that she will never be truly happy apart from you!

I pray she will comprehend that she doesn't have to stay stuck in old ways, because real progress is possible with you. You came "to proclaim freedom for the captives and release from darkness for the prisoners" (Isaiah 61:1).

When "sin is crouching" at her heart's door and "desires to have" her (Genesis 4:7), I pray she will let you answer the door and conquer it through your strength.

Set her free, Jesus—free to live for what makes you happy! Break any chains that bind her so she may follow you, rejoicing. When the angels sing, may she sing too.

May she live in such a way that you'll love to bless her. You "will withhold no good thing from those who do what is right" (Psalm 84:11[1]).

May she know the soul-satisfying sight of old sins in the rearview mirror, fading in the distance . . . and gone for good.

Then she will see the land of your promise and peace ahead, nearer and brighter every day.

KNOCK, KNOCK

I correct and discipline everyone I love. So be diligent and
turn from your indifference. Look! I stand at the door
and knock. If you hear my voice and open the door, I will
come in, and we will share a meal together as friends.

REVELATION 3:19–20[1]

Your Word tells us that *you* are "near" (Philippians 4:5), but
sometimes *we* can be so far away!

You know better than anyone how easily we're distracted. No
matter how much we love you, we can always love you more.

So today I pray you'll protect _____ from indifference
and help him to keep his focus on you.

May he "never be lacking in zeal" and keep his "spiritual
fervor," loving and "serving" you (Romans 12:11) all his life.

May you be his "first love" (Revelation 2:4[3])—his highest
priority.

When you said, "I stand at the door and knock" (3:20), you
were talking to people in the church! They were saying, "I am
rich. I have everything I want. I don't need a thing!" (v. 17[1]).

But because of their love of material things, they were spiri-
tually "neither hot nor cold" (v. 16[2]). They were "wretched
and miserable and poor and blind and naked," and didn't
even "realize" it (v. 17[1]).

Please keep my son "from idols" (1 John 5:21[2]) and the
indifference that creeps in when we love things too much.

Help him understand that anything that occupies his affections more than you is an idol.

I pray that nothing or no one will take the place in his heart that you deserve. Your Word teaches the hard truth that "if anyone loves the world, the love of the Father is not in him" (2:15²).

When the world tells him that he needs this or that thing to "be someone," remind him that he already has all he needs. When we receive you, we become your "children" and "heirs" (Romans 8:17¹)!

You tell us that when we "use the things of the world," we "should not become attached to them" (1 Corinthians 7:31¹). So I ask that he will hold his possessions lightly and use them for you.

May he comprehend that every good thing he enjoys is a gift from you, and praise you for it.

Help him understand that it is "better to have little" and be devoted to you "than to have great treasure and inner turmoil" (Proverbs 15:16¹). Only you can fill the emptiness inside!

So I pray that when my child hears you knocking at his heart's door, he'll answer with love: "Come in, Lord, and make yourself at home!"

HOPEFUL

Peter's Angel?

No one has yet believed in God and the Kingdom
of God, no one has yet heard about the realm of
the resurrected, and not been homesick from that
hour, waiting and looking forward joyfully.

DIETRICH BONHOEFFER

Sometimes when God answers prayer, we have trouble
believing it.

Peter's story comes to mind. The early church was under
heavy persecution in Jerusalem. Herod Agrippa had just
executed the apostle James and also arrested Peter (Acts
12:2–3). Herod wasn't about to let his prized prisoner get
away—Peter was "guarded by four squads of four soldiers
each" (v. 4). But the night before he was to stand trial, "the
church was earnestly praying to God for him" (v. 5).

God sent an angel to set Peter free. But Peter "had no
idea that what the angel was doing was really happening; he

189

thought he was seeing a vision" (v. 9). And when he got to the door of the house where the church was praying, Rhoda, who answered the knock, was so excited that she didn't even let him in. When she told the others, "Peter is at the door!" they answered, "You're out of your mind" (vv. 14–15). But when she "kept insisting," they said, "It must be his angel." The meaning of that comment isn't certain—they might have thought it was Peter's guardian angel. Meanwhile, Peter "kept on knocking" (v. 16).

The brouhaha that is this story gives me hope. It helps me see that even the first Christians sometimes didn't recognize an answer to prayer when it was standing right in front of them. There have been too many times in my life where I've prayed about something and then, when it happened, I forgot I'd asked for it. Or, like the people praying for Peter, I tried to explain away the answer. Still, "the Spirit helps us in our weakness" (Romans 8:26). I take comfort in the fact that God answers prayer even when our asking is less than perfect. And He's patient with us when it takes a while for us to recognize what He has done.

Well over a year after God freed my son from the prison of substance abuse, I was still deeply worried about the possibility of his falling back into it. Though I had seen God work in his life in a powerful way—though I had seen him return to his childhood faith—I kept looking for something bad to happen. "Remember," I warned him one day, "we have an adversary who is powerful."

Geoff looked me in the eye, and his response was direct. "You're right, Dad. The devil has power. But he has no authority."

In that moment I knew that my son was in God's hands, and that God could be trusted with the outcome. "All authority in heaven and on earth has been given" to Jesus (Matthew 28:18).

How good it is to know, as David put it, that "the LORD

is like a father to his children, tender and compassionate" (Psalm 103:13[1]). Because He is, we can pray with faith and be encouraged that He will answer in His time and way.

In the following pages you'll find prayers to send ahead to those places in our children's lives where mistakes are made and worry and discouragement take their toll. Even there, Jesus is Lord. Lord over our mistakes and sins, our stumbling faith, and the brokenness that results. And because He *is* Lord, we always have something to look forward to.

We can look forward to Him.

YES!

For all of God's promises have been fulfilled in Christ with
a resounding "Yes!" And through Christ, our "Amen"
(which means "Yes") ascends to God for his glory.

2 CORINTHIANS 1:20[1]

Father, when I think about the times I've had to tell my child
no (for good reasons), I praise you for when you told us
yes—for the best reason of all.

Jesus is your yes to us! "No matter how many promises"
you've made, "they are 'Yes'" in Him (2 Corinthians 1:20).

You've given us your "very great and precious promises, so
that through them" we "may participate in the divine nature,
having escaped the corruption in the world caused by evil
desires" (2 Peter 1:4).

Your goodness amazes me! You've "given us everything we
need for a godly life" (v. 3).

So I pray that you, "the source of hope, will fill" _____
"completely with joy and peace" as she trusts in you (Romans 15:13[1]). Then she "will overflow with confident hope
through the power of the Holy Spirit."

When she asks, "Does God care about me?" may she sense
your Spirit whispering, "Yes, I have loved you with an everlasting love" (Jeremiah 31:3[3]).

When she wonders how you could possibly forgive her past,
may she grasp the wonder of your unconditional love: "I—yes,

I alone—will blot out your sins for my own sake and will never think of them again" (Isaiah 43:25[1]).

When she finds herself lonely or discouraged, may your presence in her heart affirm, "I, yes I, am the one who comforts you" (51:12[1]).

And when the world tries to tell her there's another way, may she know that "there is no other God—there never has been, and there never will be" (43:10[1]). May she know your assurance: "I, yes I, am the LORD, and there is no other Savior" (v. 11[1]).

I praise you, Jesus, for what you have done! Even though we "were once far away from" the Father, "separated from him" by our "evil thoughts and actions," we've been "reconciled" through your death on the cross (Colossians 1:21–22[1]). We've been brought "into his own presence," where we are "holy and blameless" as we "stand before him without a single fault."

May my daughter know that your name is "the hope of all the world" (Matthew 12:21[1])!

I pray she'll "hold tightly without wavering to the hope we affirm," because you "can be trusted to keep" your promise (Hebrews 10:23[1]).

Because you've said yes to her in all these things, may she joyfully say yes to you!

ANGEL BY THE HAND

The angels urged Lot, saying, "Hurry! Take your
wife and your two daughters who are here, or you
will be swept away. . . ." When he hesitated, the
men grasped his hand . . . and led them safely out
of the city, for the LORD was merciful to them.

GENESIS 19:15–16

Thank you for the way you saved Lot, Lord.

He was living in Sodom with evil all around, but he still didn't want to leave. So you sent your angels to pull him and his family out of harm's way.

When I think of the close calls in my life, I wonder how many times you've done that for me.

I'll never know that number this side of heaven, but I know this: your Word says that Abraham "drew near" to you interceding for Lot (Genesis 18:23²) before the angels "grasped" him by the hand (19:16).

So today I pray for your angels to protect my child.

"Are not all angels ministering spirits sent to serve those who will inherit salvation?" (Hebrews 1:14).

I especially pray for those moments when my child—like Lot—doesn't have wisdom to get out of harm's way.

Help him, Lord! Send your angels to grab him by the hand and lead him to where he needs to be.

May _____ run to you and "make" you his "refuge" (Psalm 91:9[1]). If we make you, "the Most High," our shelter, "no evil will conquer" us, because you "will order" your angels "to protect" us (vv. 9–11[1]).

Father, you tell us, "I will rescue those who love me. I will protect those who trust in my name. When they call on me, I will answer; I will be with them in trouble. I will rescue and honor them. I will reward them with a long life and give them my salvation" (vv. 14–16[1]).

Yes, Lord! May he trust you and call on you, understanding that you alone can save us.

You are trustworthy. Because "it is impossible" for you "to lie," when we run to you for "refuge," we have "strong encouragement" and can "hold fast" to "hope" (Hebrews 6:18[2]).

Jesus, I pray he will have the "knowledge of the truth that leads to godliness" and a faith that rests "in the hope of eternal life" (Titus 1:1–2).

If he acknowledges you before others, you will even "acknowledge" him "before the angels" (Luke 12:8[2])!

May your angels know him well, Lord. Not for messes they've yanked him out of, but because of his love for you.

You've "gone into heaven" and are "at God's right hand—with angels, authorities and powers in submission" to you (1 Peter 3:22).

Please watch over my child wherever he goes.

WALKING THE WATERS OF WORRY

Then Peter got down out of the boat, walked on the water
and came toward Jesus. But when he saw the wind, he was
afraid and, beginning to sink, cried out, "Lord, save me!"
Immediately Jesus reached out his hand and caught him.

MATTHEW 14:29–31

I would have done the same thing Peter did, Lord.

As long as he had his eyes on you, everything was fine.

But it didn't take much for him to be distracted—just "the
wind" (Matthew 14:30). As soon as he started worrying about
it, "Peter (which means 'rock')" (16:18[1]) sank like a stone.

I've walked in his footsteps—just not on water.

Even though you tell us, "Do not worry about tomorrow"
(6:34[3]), sometimes it's hard for me not to do that as a parent.

But you were right there for Peter. "Immediately" you "reached
out" your hand and "caught him" (14:31).

Thank you that we can call out to you with our worries,
Lord. Your Word tells me I can "give all" my "worries and
cares" to you, because you care for us (1 Peter 5:7[1]). Peter
wrote that!

You have everything I need in your hands, and I need you
most of all.

Through your power to answer prayer, you can change the most challenging circumstances and bring good from them that we never thought possible.

I pray that _____ will learn this and know your peace, Jesus.

When, like Martha, she's "worried and upset about many things" (Luke 10:41), please help her find "what is better" (v. 42)—time spent at your feet.

It was prophesied about you, "He will be our peace" (Micah 5:5).

You are my peace, Jesus! And I pray that you'll be hers as well. Please give us both more awareness of your Spirit so that we live in your peace more and more.

I pray that you'll "increase our faith" (Luke 17:5[2]) so that when difficulties come, we'll trust you to be just as faithful in the future as you've been in the past.

You promised in your Word, "I the LORD do not change" (Malachi 3:6). You will be faithful to us just like you were to others in the past.

"Sovereign LORD, you are God! Your covenant is trustworthy" (2 Samuel 7:28). "You faithfully answer our prayers with awesome deeds, O God our savior" (Psalm 65:5[1]).

Peter called out, "Lord, save me!" (Matthew 14:30) and you reached out your hand and pulled him up.

Save us from the waters of worry, Jesus, and draw us near to yourself.

I praise you that now, just as then, your arm "is not too short to save" (Isaiah 59:1)!

STORMS

There is no one like the God of Israel.
He rides across the heavens to help you,
across the skies in majestic splendor.

DEUTERONOMY 33:26[1]

Storms can be so scary, Lord.

There's so much power in them. They make us feel so small.

I think of the times when thunder rolled and my child jumped out of his bed and into mine. He wanted to get close enough to hear my heartbeat, just to feel safe.

But I also think of the time you "rebuked the wind and said to the waves, 'Quiet! Be still!' Then the wind died down and it was completely calm" (Mark 4:39). The disciples "were terrified and asked each other, 'Who is this? Even the wind and the waves obey him!'" (v. 41).

Your power amazes me, Lord. So does your heart!

You are "the LORD Almighty" (1 Samuel 4:4), who "makes the clouds his chariot and rides on the wings of the wind" (Psalm 104:3).

But you also ride "across the heavens to help" us (Deuteronomy 33:26[1]). You are "the compassionate and gracious God, slow to anger, abounding in love and faithfulness, maintaining love to thousands, and forgiving wickedness, rebellion and sin" (Exodus 34:6–7).

I praise you because you are Lord over every storm that will ever occur in my child's life.

Please speak to the storms when they rage and he's frightened, but also speak to his heart. You're able to calm the storms within, and when they come, I pray he'll hear your voice saying, "Peace, be still" (Mark 4:39[3]).

When life's troubles raged around David, he wrote, "Oh, that I had the wings of a dove! I would fly away and be at rest. . . . I would hurry to my place of shelter, far from the tempest and storm" (Psalm 55:6, 8).

Be my son's shelter too, Lord! May he always "take refuge in the shelter of your wings" (61:4).

What's a storm to you? "The billowing clouds are" simply "the dust beneath" your "feet" (Nahum 1:3[1]).

Thank you that my son will never encounter a difficulty you can't handle.

No storm could ever be a match for you. Nothing is stronger than you, Lord, and there's "no one greater" (Hebrews 6:13).

So I pray my son will always know that your "name" is "a fortified tower; the righteous run to it and are safe" (Proverbs 18:10).

"When the storms of life come, the wicked are whirled away, but the godly have a lasting foundation" (10:25[1]).

May he always have a firm and safe foundation for his life, Jesus, because you are his "cornerstone" (Ephesians 2:20[2]).

UP WORDS

Why am I discouraged?
Why is my heart so sad?
I will put my hope in God!
I will praise him again—
my Savior and my God!

PSALM 43:5[1]

Sometimes my child feels low, and my heart goes out to him.

How I wish I could reach inside his spirit and lift him up!

But only you can do that, Lord. You can touch his heart and "put a new song" in his mouth, "a song of praise" to you (Psalm 40:3[2]).

I understand that sometimes "suffering" is "good" for us, because it causes us "to pay attention" to you (119:71[1]).

Your Word shows us where to turn when we're down: "Why am I discouraged? Why is my heart so sad? I will put my hope" in you (43:5[1]). "I will praise" you again—"my Savior and my God!"

Father, I pray that you'll help _____ to do what David did. When he was "greatly distressed" and others around him were "bitter in soul," David "strengthened himself" in you, "his God" (1 Samuel 30:6[2]).

May _____ run to you when it feels like the world is crumbling around him.

One day, "the earth will wear out like a garment," but your "salvation will last forever," and your "righteousness will never fail" (Isaiah 51:6).

When he asks, "Where does my help come from?" may his heart answer, "My help comes from the LORD, the Maker of heaven and earth" (Psalm 121:1–2).

Turn his eyes to you and help him learn to say, "Though I sit in darkness, the LORD will be my light" (Micah 7:8[1]).

"Light shines on the righteous and joy on the upright in heart" (Psalm 97:11).

When we learn to take our minds off our problems and place them on you, you lift us up. "The cheerful of heart has a continual feast" (Proverbs 15:15[2]). Please help him to feast on your goodness!

Like Joshua, may he sense your Spirit telling him, "Do not be discouraged, for the LORD your God will be with you wherever you go" (Joshua 1:9).

A man who needed you was told once, "Cheer up! . . . He's calling you!" (Mark 10:49).

Please "encourage" his heart and "strengthen" him "in every good deed and word" (2 Thessalonians 2:17).

Lift him up, Lord, and hold him close. You are "close to the brokenhearted," and you save "those who are crushed in spirit" (Psalm 34:18). You give us "eternal encouragement and good hope" (2 Thessalonians 2:16).

May my son be eternally encouraged in you! Even though we "may have many troubles" in this life (Psalm 34:19), you are greater still. And in the end, you will deliver us "from them all."

SLEEPING BEAUTY

My help comes from the LORD,
the Maker of heaven and earth.
He will not let your foot slip—
he who watches over you will not slumber;
indeed, he who watches over Israel
will neither slumber nor sleep.

PSALM 121:2–4

There are few things more beautiful than a sleeping child. How I loved to watch her sleep, Father!

Sometimes I'd stand there, caught up in the wonder you had blessed us with, dreaming of all she would be.

Do you look on us the same way, Abba?

You "decided in advance to adopt us" as your children (Ephesians 1:5[1]) through your precious Son.

Your desire is for us to be "blameless and pure," shining "like stars in the sky" (Philippians 2:15).

You stand there watching "over" us and "neither slumber nor sleep" (Psalm 121:4), gazing on us with a love deeper than we can comprehend.

You, "the everlasting God" (Isaiah 40:28[2]), went to the grave and back to bring us home to yourself!

You said your people are your "most precious possession" (Zechariah 2:8[1]).

When you look on my sleeping child, Jesus, what is it you see?

"No one can fathom" your "understanding" (Isaiah 40:28). You see good things yet to be awakened within her that no one else sees.

I praise you for making us "heirs having the hope of eternal life" (Titus 3:7).

You not only treasure her as she is; you see what she will be!

You said that one day "the righteous will shine like the sun in the kingdom of their Father" (Matthew 13:43[2]). You can already see her there, standing in "the Holy City, the new Jerusalem" (Revelation 21:2), shining brightly in the salvation you have won for us.

But before she gets there, she must grow in the grace that "teaches us to say 'No' to ungodliness and worldly passions, and to live self-controlled, upright and godly lives in this present age, while we wait for the blessed hope"—your "appearing," our "great God and Savior" (Titus 2:12–13).

So your Word tells us to "wake up," because "our salvation is nearer now than when we first believed" (Romans 13:11[1]).

We are only becoming aware of all that you are, all that you are calling us to be!

And your Spirit encourages us, "Awake, O sleeper, and arise from the dead, and Christ will shine on you" (Ephesians 5:14[2]).

"Let the light of your face shine" on her, Lord (Psalm 4:6), and awaken your hope within.

May your every dream for my child come true. Then she will "walk in the light of your presence" (89:15) forever!

READY OR NOT

So you also must be ready, because the Son of Man
will come at an hour when you do not expect him.

MATTHEW 24:44

Sometimes when we'd play games as kids, we'd say, "Ready
or not, here I come!"

Please get him ready, Jesus.

Ready for what really matters.

Ready for "the day of" your return (Joel 2:1).

You taught about it often, telling us to "be ready" because you
will come when we "do not expect" you (Matthew 24:44).

And you're not playing games.

Your Word is very clear on that. It tells us that day "will come
like a thief. The heavens will disappear with a roar; the elements will be destroyed by fire, and the earth and everything
done in it will be laid bare" (2 Peter 3:10).

Oh, Lord, what a day that will be! "While people are saying,
'There is peace and security,' then sudden destruction will
come" (1 Thessalonians 5:3²).

Because we "do not know" when you "will come," I ask
that you help both me and my child to "keep watch" (Matthew 24:42).

May even the clouds remind us, because you said that in
days to come we "will see the Son of Man sitting at the

right hand of the Mighty One" and "coming on the clouds of heaven" (26:64[4]).

Thank you that we don't have to "be surprised when the day" comes (1 Thessalonians 5:4[1]); we can even look forward to it!

When you "appear a second time," you will "save those who are eagerly waiting" for you (Hebrews 9:28[2]).

Father, I praise you because you "chose to save us through our Lord Jesus Christ, not to pour out" your "anger on us" (1 Thessalonians 5:9[1]).

"He died for us" so that we "may live together with him" (v. 10)! May my child always be aware that you are near, Jesus, and "stay alert and be clearheaded" (v. 6[1]).

May he "be careful" so that his heart is not "weighed down with carousing, drunkenness and the anxieties of life" (Luke 21:34). May his heart be lifted by the hope of being with you.

I pray that the cry of his heart will be, "I look to the LORD for help. I wait confidently for God to save me, and my God will certainly hear me" (Micah 7:7[1]).

I pray my child will "long for" you (Psalm 130:6[1]), Jesus!

You said that "no one can come" to you "unless the Father who sent" you "draws them" (John 6:44[1]). Please draw him near, Father!

Then, even on this earth, he'll be among the "citizens of heaven," ready and "eagerly waiting" for your Son "to return as our Savior" (Philippians 3:20[1]).

OVERCOMING

Love When We're over Our Heads

Daddy . . . who was praying for me Tuesday night?

CHRISSY CYMBALA TOLEDO

"God will never allow you to go through more than you can bear."

You hear people say it all the time, and they mean it kindly. It's something you hear when you're in a hard place, and it's intended as a reminder of God's faithfulness. But comforting as those words may seem, there's a problem with them.

God never made that promise.

Here's what His Word actually says:

> No temptation has overtaken you except what is common to mankind. And God is faithful; *he will not let you be tempted beyond what you can bear.* But when you are tempted, he

will also provide a way out so that you can
endure it. (1 Corinthians 10:13)

It may be the most misquoted verse in Scripture—and the difference between the two thoughts shouldn't be missed. God promises us a way out when we're *tempted*, but that specific promise can't be applied to all of life's problems. When we think that way, we set ourselves up for a painful misunderstanding. What do you do in those crushing moments when life's circumstances are more than you can bear? Where do you turn? Do you give up on God and decide that He's no longer faithful? Do you stop praying because it "didn't work," or think that God has given up on you?

The hard truth is that life sometimes *is* more than we can bear. But we were never intended to bear it alone. God *has* promised, "Never will I leave you; never will I forsake you" (Hebrews 13:5). Jesus said, "I am with you *always*" (Matthew 28:20). Sometimes life's circumstances will drive us to our knees. But it's there that we're in the best position for God to help us.

We can also be tempted to believe that "God helps those who help themselves"—but that isn't in the Bible either. God isn't into self-reliance. He's into dependence. Jesus said of His relationship to the Father, "By myself I can do nothing" (John 5:30). He also said, "Apart from me *you* can do nothing" (15:5). It's often in the middle of our problems that a tough but comforting truth meets us. When God allows us to go through more than we can bear, we discover *how much we need Him*. When we come to the end of ourselves, we find that He is enough.

The apostle John, who as the disciple who outlived all the others was no stranger to heartache, wrote that "everyone born of God overcomes the world" (1 John 5:4). Then he added, "This is the victory that has overcome the world, *even our faith*" (v. 4). God has ways of showing His faithfulness when we're in over our heads. Not just the faithfulness of saving us from our circumstances (though He sometimes does that), but the faithfulness of meeting us in unexpected places and pouring new strength into us. As we turn to Him, He lifts us out of our self-focus and the thought that our own lives are the center of the universe, and He carries us to new places of praise. That's why David could write in the middle of an unresolved difficulty, "Praise the Lord; praise God our Savior! For each day he carries us in his arms" (Psalm 68:19[1]).

Jesus said, "In this world you will have trouble. But take heart! I have overcome the world" (John 16:33). This week we'll pray that our children will also overcome through Him. We'll ask that they may persevere in faith with "strength of character" and "confident hope of salvation" (Romans 5:3–4[1]) because they "know whom" they "have believed" (2 Timothy 1:12).

These are prayers that take the long view, seeing our children through life's adversity and all the way home.

SOMEONE WITH HIM IN THE FIRE

Then King Nebuchadnezzar leaped to his feet in amazement and asked his advisers, "Weren't there three men that we tied up and threw into the fire?" They replied, "Certainly, Your Majesty." He said, "Look! I see four men walking around in the fire, . . . and the fourth looks like a son of the gods."

DANIEL 3:24–25

Jesus, I know there will be days when _____ has to walk through fire.

Difficulties come; we are "born to trouble as surely as sparks fly upward" (Job 5:7).

I wish I could keep him from it, but I also know he'll find strength there that can be forged nowhere else. "Suffering produces perseverance; perseverance, character; and character, hope. And hope does not put us to shame," because you have "poured out" your love "into our hearts through the Holy Spirit, who has been given to us" (Romans 5:3–5).

So I ask that you'll be with him whenever he walks through fire.

You've promised your presence in the most challenging circumstances: "When you pass through the waters, I will be with you; and through the rivers, they shall not overwhelm you; when you walk through fire you shall not be burned, and the flame shall not consume you. For I am the Lord your God, the Holy One of Israel, your Savior" (Isaiah 43:2–3²).

Jesus, as almighty God you are "the same yesterday and today and forever" (Hebrews 13:8²), and your promises can be trusted!

When Nebuchadnezzar had Shadrach, Meshach, and Abednego thrown into the fire, there were "four men walking around," and "the fourth" looked like "a son of the gods" (Daniel 3:24–25). That was you, wasn't it!

You told us, "I am with you always, even to the end of the age" (Matthew 28:20³).

If you are near my child, he will be "unbound and unharmed" (Daniel 3:25).

When there is the smoke of confusion around him, may you give him all the direction he needs. I pray that his "own ears will hear" you guiding him (Isaiah 30:21¹). "Right behind" him "a voice will say, 'This is the way you should go,' whether to the right or to the left."

Your Word says, "A friend loves at all times, and a brother is born for adversity" (Proverbs 17:17²). There is no friend like you!

Your Word also says, "There is a friend who sticks closer than a brother" (18:24²). You are that friend—no one sticks closer than you.

You are Immanuel, "God with us" (Matthew 1:23)!

Thank you that you will be with my son wherever he goes.

WHEN A LAMB WIPES TEARS AWAY

To all who mourn in Israel,
he will give a crown of beauty for ashes,
a joyous blessing instead of mourning,
festive praise instead of despair.

ISAIAH 61:3[1]

My child's tears touch my heart, Lord.

But I'm moved by the fact that they touch yours even more. Your Word says "you keep track" of all our sorrows (Psalm 56:8[1]). "You have collected" all our "tears in your bottle. You have recorded each one in your book."

Nothing escapes you! Not even the slightest sigh.

Thank you for your tender love. "How kind" you are (116:5[1])! "How good" you are. You're "so merciful."

So I pray _____ will know the comfort you can give her heart. You even tell us that when we mourn, we're somehow "blessed" (Matthew 5:4[2])—because there is a comfort only you can give.

How you love your people, Jesus!

I love the promise in your Word that you will one day "wipe every tear" from our eyes (Revelation 21:4[1]). "There will be no more death or sorrow or crying or pain." All of these things will be "gone forever."

You, "the Lamb on the throne," will be our "Shepherd," and you'll lead us to "springs of life-giving water" (7:17[1]).

I wish I could always be there to wipe my child's tears, but I know there'll be tears my hands can't touch.

So I place her in your hands and thank you for your perfect love. You are "the Lamb of God, who takes away the sin of the world!" (John 1:29[2]).

You do "not treat us as our sins deserve or repay us according to our iniquities" (Psalm 103:10).

You were "pierced for our transgressions" and "crushed for our iniquities; the punishment that brought us peace was on" you, and by your "wounds we are healed" (Isaiah 53:5).

You "wept over" your people (Luke 19:41[2]) and went to the cross so that our tears may one day be no more.

By faith I see her there, standing before you on that day. A "crown of beauty" (Isaiah 61:3[1]) rests where time and care once drew their lines.

How she's grown! "Perseverance" has finished "its work" so that she is "mature and complete, not lacking anything" (James 1:4).

Your hand touches her face, and in a single motion every sorrow is swept away and only your peace remains.

This is my prayer for my daughter, Lord. May she be among "those the LORD has rescued" who return and "enter Zion with singing" (Isaiah 35:10). And may she stand in wonder before you, as she is welcomed into the "everlasting joy" of your amazing love.

WORLD'S WORST BULLY

Then there was war in heaven. . . . And the dragon lost the
battle, and he and his angels were forced out of heaven.
This great dragon—the ancient serpent called the devil . . .
was thrown down to the earth with all his angels.

REVELATION 12:7–9[1]

I can hardly wait for you to deal with the devil once and
for all, Jesus.

He's caused so much heartache! But when your kingdom
comes, that will all be behind us.

You've promised to create "a new heaven and a new earth,
where righteousness dwells"—and I am "looking forward"
to it (2 Peter 3:13)!

But until then, the world's worst bully is still on the prowl.
"He is filled with fury, because he knows that his time is
short" (Revelation 12:12). So I pray that you will protect
_____ from him.

But because of your cross, we face a defeated foe!

You "disarmed the spiritual rulers and authorities" and
"shamed them publicly" by your "victory over them on the
cross" (Colossians 2:15[1]).

Our adversary has power but no authority. "All authority
in heaven and on earth has been given" to you, Lord Jesus
(Matthew 28:18[2]).

You've even given *us* authority "to overcome all the power of the enemy" (Luke 10:19).

Even though there are battles to fight, the war is won! And those who know you can "rejoice" that their "names are written in heaven" (v. 20[2]).

I pray that _____ will have a healthy, humble understanding of all you've done so that he may not be afraid when the enemy attacks him.

May he understand that his strength to overcome is found in you. May he be among those who "listen to" your voice and "follow" you, Lord Jesus (John 10:27[1]). You have promised that "they will never perish, and no one will snatch them" out of your hand (v. 28[2]).

You are always vigilant. You neither "slumber nor sleep" (Psalm 121:4[2]).

Please help him be vigilant as well. May he be "alert and of sober mind" (1 Peter 5:8), so that he'll "not be outwitted by Satan" or "ignorant of" his schemes (2 Corinthians 2:11[2]).

Your eyes "search the whole earth in order to strengthen those whose hearts are fully committed" to you (2 Chronicles 16:9[1]). Strengthen his heart and commitment, Jesus.

The devil is no match for you! You "saw Satan fall like lightning from heaven" (Luke 10:18[2]).

I pray that my child will "resist the devil" and that the devil "will flee" from him (James 4:7). "May your Kingdom come soon" (Matthew 6:10[1]), so that every battle is won!

JUMPING FOR JOY

He will also keep you firm to the end, so that you
will be blameless on the day of our Lord Jesus
Christ. God is faithful, who has called you into
fellowship with his Son, Jesus Christ our Lord.

1 CORINTHIANS 1:8–9

Bringing up children in this world isn't easy, God.

_____ is precious to me, and I want to protect her!

But above all, I want her to be faithful. There's no greater protection than to rest "in the shadow of your wings" (Psalm 36:7²).

"*Abba*, Father" (Mark 14:36), when I think about what it was like for you to see your Son suffer for our sins, my heart hurts.

I can't imagine what you went through! I'm so sorry, but I'm also thankful—because I know you did it to rescue us.

Once you rescue us, you never leave us. You even promise to "keep" us "strong in faith to the very end" (1 Corinthians 1:8⁴).

So today I pray that my child will know the strength you can give to face anything.

Your Word tells us that "all who desire to live a godly life in Christ Jesus will be persecuted, while evil people and impostors will go on from bad to worse" (2 Timothy 3:12–13²).

I understand that because _____ believes in you, life won't always be easy. You alone know what she'll have to face, but I want to thank you for being there for her. You have "called" her into a relationship with yourself, and you are "faithful" (1 Corinthians 1:9)!

Jesus, it hurts to think of what she may face because of her faith, but I know that as she stays close to you, all will be well.

As we walk with you, you make us more like you. We are "transformed into" your "image with ever-increasing glory" through your Spirit (2 Corinthians 3:18).

You even said, "Blessed are you when people insult you, persecute you and falsely say all kinds of evil against you because of me. Rejoice and be glad, because great is your reward in heaven" (Matthew 5:11–12). You not only said to "rejoice in that day"; you also told us to "leap for joy" (Luke 6:23[2]) because the reward in heaven will be so great!

So I pray that in that moment she'll see beyond sorrow—and make the leap of faith into your joy and peace.

You, "for the joy set before" you, "endured the cross, scorning its shame, and sat down at the right hand of the throne of God" (Hebrews 12:2).

I thank you for where the road comes out, Lord. As my daughter takes up her "cross" to "follow" you (Matthew 10:38), the joy of all you are will be her best reward.

And she'll happily sit at your feet forever.

THE CROSS
AND THE FIGHT

I have fought the good fight, I have finished
the race, I have kept the faith.

2 TIMOTHY 4:7

I pray that _____ will *really* follow you, Jesus. But that
isn't easy.

You said, "If anyone would come after me, let him deny himself and take up his cross daily and follow me" (Luke 9:23[2]).

And you said that if we "refuse to take up" our crosses and
follow you, we "are not worthy" of being yours (Matthew
10:38[1]).

We can only do this if you help us. Our faith must "rest on"
your "power" (1 Corinthians 2:5).

But we also must give you nothing less than our best.

Paul's words encourage me: "I have fought the good fight, I
have finished the race" (2 Timothy 4:7).

He said he ran "with purpose in every step" and wasn't "just
shadowboxing" (1 Corinthians 9:26[1]).

He tried hard! So I ask that you help my child overcome every
obstacle he faces also, including his own will.

You said that you came "down from heaven, not to do" your
"own will but the will of him who sent" you (John 6:38[2]).
You didn't live for yourself on this earth.

Please help my son to live intentionally for you.

Jesus, you told us that if we "cling to" our lives, we "will lose" them, but if we "give up" our lives for you, we "will find" them (Matthew 10:39[1]).

You also said, "As the Father has sent me, so I am sending you" (John 20:21[1]).

So I ask that you help my child to "throw off everything that hinders and the sin that so easily entangles" and "run with perseverance the race marked out for" him (Hebrews 12:1).

May he have "patient endurance" to go the distance so that he "will continue to do" your will (10:36[1]). Then he "will receive all" that you have "promised."

May he run to you, "Jesus, the pioneer and perfecter of faith" (12:2)!

May his "soul live and praise you" (Psalm 119:175[2]), because "neither death nor life, neither angels nor demons, neither our fears for today nor our worries about tomorrow—not even the powers of hell can separate us" from your love (Romans 8:38[1]). "No power in the sky above or in the earth below . . . nothing in all creation will ever be able to separate us" from your love (v. 39[1])!

I thank you that the fight can be won, the race finished, and the faith kept, because your "faithful love endures forever" (2 Chronicles 20:21[1]).

DELIVERED

I prayed to the LORD, and he answered me.
He freed me from all my fears. . . .
In my desperation I prayed, and the LORD listened;
he saved me from all my troubles.

PSALM 34:4, 6[1]

How many times have you helped me, Lord?

You've "delivered" me "from trouble" (Proverbs 11:8[2]) again and again!

You're my "refuge and strength, an ever-present help in trouble" (Psalm 46:1). So I ask that you help my child as well.

I pray that _____ will call on you when life gets hard, Father. Your Word tells us, "Is anyone among you in trouble? Then that person should pray" (James 5:13[4]).

Even when we're surrounded on all sides, the way up is always open. You are the "One who breaks open the way" (Micah 2:13)!

Help him to learn to pray, Lord. You are "near to all who call" on you from the heart (Psalm 145:18[2]). You fulfill "the desire of those who fear" you (v. 19[2]). You hear "their cry" and save them, because you watch over "all who love" you (vv. 19–20[2]).

When we don't see trouble coming, we can still trust you to help us. "The godly may trip seven times, but they will get up again" (Proverbs 24:16[1]).

"As soon as" we pray, "you answer" us; "you encourage" us "by giving" us "strength" (Psalm 138:3[1]).

Even when our circumstances don't seem to change, we can trust that you're at work. "For you bless the godly, O LORD; you surround them with your shield of love" (5:12[1]). You turn our "darkness into light" (2 Samuel 22:29). You are "the Awesome One" (Psalm 76:11[1]).

"Great" is your "faithfulness," Lord (Lamentations 3:23[1])! Your "mercies begin afresh each morning." So I pray that each "morning" brings him "word of your unfailing love" because he puts his "trust in you" (Psalm 143:8).

When we are "overwhelmed, you alone know the way" we "should turn" (142:3[1]).

Whenever _____ is in trouble, may he "look to you for protection" and "hide beneath the shadow of your wings until the danger passes by" (57:1[1]).

"Show" him your "unfailing love and faithfulness," Father (2 Samuel 15:20[1]).

You have "rescued us from the dominion of darkness and brought us into the kingdom of the Son" you love, "in whom we have redemption, the forgiveness of sins" (Colossians 1:13–14).

May the strong cry of my son's heart be, "The Lord will deliver me from every evil attack and will bring me safely into his heavenly Kingdom. All glory to God forever and ever! Amen" (2 Timothy 4:18[1])!

"COME TO THE TABLE!"

People will come from east and west and north and south, and will take their places at the feast in the kingdom of God.

LUKE 13:29

I can see my child at that banquet, Lord.

There she is! She's beautiful, "dressed in white" (Revelation 3:4), not a single line or care on her face.

She's come to "sit down with Abraham, Isaac, and Jacob at the feast in the Kingdom of Heaven" (Matthew 8:11[1]).

So many others are there too! There's the "Roman officer" (v. 5[1]) whose faith impressed you so much, and "Lazarus" seated close to Abraham (Luke 16:23). He was poor and disregarded on this earth but in a place of honor now.

I can only imagine the talk around that table. What stories we'll hear of your faithfulness, made all the clearer once our "race" is run (2 Timothy 4:7) and we "know fully" (1 Corinthians 13:12) all you've done for us.

We "will give glory to your name forever" (Psalm 86:12[1])!

I so look forward to being there. And I pray all our family will be.

I pray that my child will "make every effort to enter through the narrow door" (Luke 13:24) that leads to the kingdom of heaven. You are "the door," Jesus (John 10:9[2]). "If anyone enters" by you, that person "will be saved."

"We are looking forward to a new heaven and a new earth, where righteousness dwells" (2 Peter 3:13), promised to all who turn from their sins and turn to you.

One day in the "new Jerusalem" (Revelation 3:12) you "will spread a wonderful feast" (Isaiah 25:6[1]). You "will remove the cloud of gloom, the shadow of death that hangs over the earth," and "will wipe away all tears" (vv. 7–8[1]).

What a day that will be! "In that day" we will proclaim, "This is our God! We trusted in him, and he saved us!" (v. 9[1]). We'll always "rejoice in the salvation" you give—an adventure in unlimited life with you that never ends.

"People will come from east and west and north and south" (Luke 13:29), and we'll praise you with a shout, "Salvation belongs to our God who sits on the throne, and to the Lamb!" (Revelation 7:10[2]).

As John heard an angel say: "Blessed are those who are invited to the wedding supper of the Lamb!" (19:9).

May my child be blessed to come to that table, Jesus.

I pray she'll know how much you love her—and be filled with so much love for you that she'll sing for joy, "He has brought me to his banquet hall, and his banner over me is love" (Song of Songs 2:4[5]).

WEEK 13

BLESSED

"It Just Keeps Getting Better"

Let none of us be content . . . until [Jesus] has received
our children, and has so blessed them that we are
sure that they have entered the Kingdom of God.

CHARLES HADDON SPURGEON

"Say goodbye to a good night's sleep!"
"There goes your freedom!"
"Just you wait! Your life is really going to change."
When our baby girl was born, we got all kinds of advice.
But one simple sentence stood head and shoulders above
the rest.

It came from Mal King, an FBI-trained criminal investi-
gator who also had daughters. One day I shared with him
some little thing my three-month-old had done. He smiled
broadly and said, "It just keeps getting better."

Mal was more than an optimist. He had seen a lot of the
dark side of life and could have viewed things very differently.

But he trusted God deeply—and that confidence hung in the air with his words. His was a statement of faith I would never forget.

"It just keeps getting better." Learn to rest in God and you have something to look forward to, no matter what life may hold. A blessed life can't be measured by possessions or health or a few short years when things go well on this earth. When you're truly blessed, eternity opens wide before you with hope—the very presence of the living Lord Jesus—that presses in on the moment. "Christ in you, the hope of glory" (Colossians 1:27) is how the apostle Paul described it. And when our sons and daughters take Jesus to heart, they live large in the big life that only God can give them—"life by the power of his name" (John 20:31[1]).

The prayers in these last pages are written so that our children may be blessed with the "all-surpassing" life God gives (2 Corinthians 4:7) and finish well. You'll find prayers for their relationships with God and others, for purpose and direction in life, and for their eternal destiny. As you pray, I hope you'll keep in mind the moments when Jesus "took the children in his arms, placed his hands on them and blessed them" (Mark 10:16). Whatever your children's (or grandchildren's) ages, imagine bringing them to Jesus so He may touch them and "they may take hold of the life that is truly life" (1 Timothy 6:19).

We can think of so many ways we want our children to be blessed, but Jesus knows how to bless them best for an eternal lifetime. C. S. Lewis described heaven as "the Great Story which no one on earth has read: which goes on for ever: in which every chapter is better than the one before."[12] These are prayers that the hope of heaven will shine into our children's souls even now, and be the story of their lives forever.

FOREVER BLESSED

He said to them, "Let the little children come to me, and
do not hinder them, for the kingdom of God belongs
to such as these. . . ." And he took the children in his
arms, placed his hands on them and blessed them.

MARK 10:14, 16

I can see my son standing right in front of you, Jesus.

You have both hands on his shoulders and are smiling . . .
looking in his eyes and blessing him.

What more could my child possibly need than that? So by
faith I bring him to you and ask that you bless him.

May he hear your "still small voice" (1 Kings 19:12[3]) speaking to him about all that you are, convicting him of his sin
and leading him "into all truth" (John 16:13[1]), closer to you.

I never want to do anything to "hinder" him from coming
to you (Matthew 19:14). Where I have "hidden faults"
(Psalm 19:12[2]) that I'm not even aware of, don't let them
get in the way!

"I am your servant; give me discernment that I may understand" (119:125) what you want me to do to help him know
and love you.

"You are the God of great wonders! You demonstrate your
awesome power" (77:14[1]) in amazing ways.

You have even hidden spiritual truths "from the wise and
learned, and revealed them to little children" (Luke 10:21).

I ask that my son will "receive" you and "the Kingdom of God like a child" (18:17[1]), so that he may enjoy you forever.

Just as he once ran to me whenever he had a need, I pray he'll learn to "run to you" (Isaiah 55:5[3]), talking and listening to you.

Yet it's human nature to follow our own wisdom. "All of us, like sheep, have strayed away. We have left" your "paths to follow our own" (53:6[1]). We are lost without you!

But with you, we are "washed," "sanctified," and "justified in the name of the Lord Jesus Christ and by the Spirit of our God" (1 Corinthians 6:11[2]).

So here is my child, Lord. I bring him before you today.

Please touch him and bless him in whatever ways he needs most, so that there may be no doubt that your "hand" is "with" him (Acts 11:21).

May your hand be on him wherever he goes! May he know your peace in his soul and live each day in friendship with you.

Please keep blessing my child beyond my years, until we stop counting years and they are no more.

"When you grant a blessing, O LORD, it is an eternal blessing!" (1 Chronicles 17:27[1]).

May my child be forever blessed!

WHAT TO WEAR

Therefore, as God's chosen people, holy and
dearly loved, clothe yourselves with compassion,
kindness, humility, gentleness and patience.

COLOSSIANS 3:12

"I don't have anything to wear!"

How many times have you heard us say that, Father, even
though we have clothes to spare?

I want to pray about what my child wears. But that's about
so much more than clothes!

You want us to "walk as children of light" (Ephesians 5:8[2])
and "clothe" ourselves "with compassion, kindness, humility, gentleness and patience" (Colossians 3:12).

You want us to dress like you.

You are "a God of compassion and mercy, slow to get angry
and filled with unfailing love and faithfulness" (Psalm 86:15[1]).

"O LORD my God, how great you are! You are robed with
honor and majesty. You are dressed in a robe of light"
(104:1–2[1]).

So I pray that _____ will be dressed in the beauty of your
"love and mercy" (Isaiah 63:9).

I pray she'll "have compassion" on those in need (Matthew
15:32) as you do, Jesus, and that she'll act with kindness in
ways that resemble you.

Your Word tells us to "sympathize with each other," to "love each other as brothers and sisters," to "be tenderhearted," and to "keep a humble attitude" (1 Peter 3:8[1]).

You want us to "put on" our "new nature, and be renewed" as we "learn to know" you and "become like" you (Colossians 3:10[1]).

Forgive us for being distracted by things that you promised to take care of: "'What will we eat? What will we drink? What will we wear?' These things dominate the thoughts of unbelievers," but you know all our "needs" (Matthew 6:31–32[1]).

Those who love you will one day be dressed in "the finest of pure white linen," which "represents the good deeds of" your "holy people" (Revelation 19:8[1]).

I pray my child will dress herself in those deeds now and "put on righteousness" as her "clothing" (Job 29:14). I pray that she'll "dress modestly, with decency and propriety" (1 Timothy 2:9).

Please give her the grace and willingness to "put on" her "new nature, created to be like" you—"truly righteous and holy" (Ephesians 4:24[1]).

You said, "Blessed are all who are watching" for you, "who keep their clothing ready" (Revelation 16:15[1]).

Cover her with your righteousness, Jesus! May her life be "hidden with" you "in God," so that she "also will appear with" you "in glory" (Colossians 3:3–4).

FATHER'S EYES

And afterward,
I will pour out my Spirit on all people.
Your sons and daughters will prophesy,
your old men will dream dreams,
your young men will see visions.

JOEL 2:28

Your dreams for _____ are so much greater than mine, Father.

I have a lifetime in view, but you see from here to eternity.

I "see" only "dimly" (1 Corinthians 13:12[2]), and my vision is tainted with self and sin.

Your sight is perfect. You see who _____ will be ages from now beyond time, when you've given him "a new name" (Revelation 2:17) and made him what he was always meant to be.

"What we will be has not yet been made known" (1 John 3:2). You alone know that! "But we know that when Christ appears, we shall be like him."

Your Spirit makes known to us what "he receives from" you (John 16:15[1]) and "has revealed" to us (1 Corinthians 2:10) that you have beautiful things planned for those who love you.

Because "the Spirit searches all things, even the deep things of God" (v. 10), I pray you will lead my son into new heights and depths of understanding how wonderful you are.

May he be caught up in your vision for his life, Father. The world has so many counterfeits; may he have "the mind of Christ" (v. 16) so he may understand your will for him.

May he "follow the way of love and eagerly desire gifts of the Spirit" (14:1).

Please help him to "walk in obedience" to you and "keep" your "commands" so that you "will bless" him (Deuteronomy 30:16) as long as he lives.

Should you bless him with many years, may his vision increase!

I pray his eyes won't be fixed on the glory days of his youth; instead, "show" him "your glory" (Exodus 33:18).

May he "dream dreams" (Joel 2:28) of how good it will be to see you "face to face" (Numbers 12:8) and live in the beauty of your presence.

What better thought could fill his mind than you?

What earthly dream could he long for that could give him more joy than you?

You are "the eternal God" (Romans 16:26). You are "great" and "most worthy of praise" (1 Chronicles 16:25).

You do "not take" your "eyes off the righteous"; you "exalt them forever" (Job 36:7).

How good you are! How amazingly kind you are to save us.

"May those who long for your saving help always say, 'The LORD is great!'" (Psalm 70:4).

"LOVES ME, LOVES ME NOT"

All night long on my bed I looked for the one my heart loves.
SONG OF SONGS 3:1

Today I pray for the love of my child's life.

I'm not only thinking about who she may marry. I'm thinking about the only one who can make her relationships work—you!

Your Word tells us, "Above all else, guard your heart, for everything you do flows from it" (Proverbs 4:23).

How quickly the waters of that spring are muddied when we don't let in your love. But you promised that "rivers of living water will flow" from the "heart" of "anyone who believes" in you (John 7:38[1]).

So, above all, I pray you will be the love of her life.

I pray she won't need a man to make her happy; may she find her "heart's desire" (Psalm 20:4[2]) in you.

May she be so close to you that she'll seek your guidance and blessing in every relationship in her life. "The desire of the righteous ends only in good" (Proverbs 11:23[2])!

Help her choose her relationships wisely.

When she's attracted to someone, may she reach beyond her human desires and ask, "Is this what God wants?"

It is a hard thing to pray, "Not my will, but yours, be done" (Luke 22:42[2]). But if she does, Jesus, she'll be following your example.

The human heart is so fickle; it loves and then loves not. But you can "set" her "heart on the right path" (Proverbs 23:19).

"True wisdom" is "found in" you; "counsel and understanding" are yours (Job 12:13[1]). You are the "Wonderful Counselor" (Isaiah 9:6[2])!

If it's your desire that she be single, may she be strong and joyful, doing your work and thinking about "how to please" you (1 Corinthians 7:32[1]).

If she "should marry" (v. 9), please lead her to "a good person" (Proverbs 13:22) who loves you and loves her deeply. May he treat her like "a treasure" (18:22[1])!

Help them to "submit to one another out of reverence" for you (Ephesians 5:21) so that they will live in your peace.

May they "remain faithful to one another in marriage" (Hebrews 13:4[1]) so that they will be protected from the heartache and destruction of sin.

If it is your will, please bless them with children. May they know you and love you too! "Children are a gift" from you (Psalm 127:3[1]).

You invented love and know how to make it work. May she long for you "above all" (John 3:31)!

May you be the one her "heart loves" (Song of Songs 3:1).

SO LOVED

For God so loved the world that he gave his
one and only Son, that whoever believes in him
shall not perish but have eternal life.

JOHN 3:16

Sometimes when I look at my child, I wonder how I could love him more.

I love him so much it hurts, Father!

No one understands that better than you.

"This is how" you showed your "love among us": you sent your "one and only Son into the world that we might live through him" (1 John 4:9).

"He personally carried our sins in his body on the cross so that we can be dead to sin and live for what is right" (1 Peter 2:24[1]). For "by his wounds" we "are healed."

You "so loved" us that you "gave" us your "one and only Son" (John 3:16), even when we had "rebelled against you" (Psalm 5:10[2]).

"So loved" (John 3:16). I love those words, Father!

We are *so loved*, and I pray _____ will understand that.

Please use me in any way you desire to share your perfect love with him.

I think of what Mary told the angel sent to announce Jesus's birth: "I am the Lord's servant" (Luke 1:38).

"I *am* your servant," Lord (Psalm 119:125). Please "give me discernment that I may understand" whatever you want me to do.

Since you "so loved us, we also ought to love one another" (1 John 4:11²). Help me to love him with the love you give.

"Your love, LORD, reaches to the heavens," and "your faithfulness to the skies" (Psalm 36:5).

"Your love" for us "is very great. You have rescued" us "from the depths of death" (86:13¹), and I want to praise you always for what you've done!

"It is good to praise" you, "O Most High" (92:1). "It is good to proclaim your unfailing love in the morning" and "your faithfulness in the evening" (v. 2¹).

Help me to love you fully and faithfully so that my child will be drawn to your loving presence through me.

There are so many counterfeit notions of what love is in the world; please let my child see the real thing—your love.

There is nothing like your love! "Your love is better than life" (63:3)—and stronger than death.

Your love meets my child's deepest need.

May you lead his heart "into a full understanding and expression of the love of God and the patient endurance that comes from Christ" (2 Thessalonians 3:5¹).

HOME

Praise be to the God and Father of our Lord Jesus
Christ, who has blessed us in the heavenly realms
with every spiritual blessing in Christ.

EPHESIANS 1:3

Home at last.

That's the single greatest blessing I ask for _____, Father.

I pray that when her "race" is "run," she'll have "run in such
a way as to get the prize" (1 Corinthians 9:24).

You are her heart's true home. You made us to love you
forever!

What "glorious grace" you've "poured out" on those "who
belong" to your "dear Son" (Ephesians 1:6[1]). You've already
"blessed us in the heavenly realms with every spiritual blessing in Christ" (v. 3).

We're not home yet, but even now you're with us, giving us
strength we wouldn't otherwise have—because you give "the
Spirit without limit" (John 3:34).

What a "beautiful inheritance" (Psalm 16:6[2]) you have prepared for those who follow you! "Whoever believes in the
Son has eternal life" (John 3:36[2]).

So I pray that my daughter will follow you all the way home,
Jesus.

Please rescue her from this world "out of the goodness of
your love" (Psalm 109:21).

Help me to "keep on praying" for her as long as I live, so that through my prayers I may help her "live a life worthy" of your "call" (2 Thessalonians 1:11[1]).

"As for me and my family, we will serve" you (Joshua 24:15[1])!

Your Word promises that "the children of your servants will live in your presence" (Psalm 102:28). I am your servant, Father!

You bless "the home of the righteous" (Proverbs 3:33), and I pray ours will be that. May we walk by faith "from generation to generation" (Exodus 3:15).

You "gave" your "life to free us from every kind of sin, to cleanse us, and to make us" your "very own people, totally committed" (Titus 2:14[1]).

May _____ "remain true to" you "with all" her heart (Acts 11:23)!

I pray she will "prove" herself by her "purity," her "understanding," her "patience," her "kindness"—by "the Holy Spirit within" her and by her "sincere love" for you and for others (2 Corinthians 6:6[1]).

May you "be honored because of the way" she lives (2 Thessalonians 1:12[1]), Jesus!

Until the day she is home at last, the race done and the battle won, may she "make every effort to be found spotless, blameless and at peace with" you (2 Peter 3:14).

May her heart be in heaven before she ever gets there, longing for home and looking forward to you!

CONCLUSION

Love beyond Life

For this reason I kneel before the Father, from whom
every family in heaven and on earth derives its name. I
pray that out of his glorious riches he may strengthen
you with power through his Spirit in your inner being,
so that Christ may dwell in your hearts through faith.

EPHESIANS 3:14–17

"Mom, the good news is I've become a Christian."
Sarah looked intently at her son. "And the bad
news?"

The story that followed was one no parent hopes to hear.
Sarah's son had been caught smuggling drugs in the trunk of
his car across state lines. There was little doubt he would be
found guilty, and it looked like Robert would go to prison
for years.

Sarah had done her best to raise her son to believe in Jesus.
Every Sunday of his young life found them at church, but
the lure of wealth and the world pulled him to a place Sarah
never imagined. Still, she placed Robert in God's hands day
by day and loved him through her prayers. After he repented,

239

Sarah still grieved the mistakes he had made, but she was grateful to see a sincere new faith in him.

When the case against Robert was dismissed on a technicality, no one was more surprised than Sarah. And no one was more pleased as her son continued steadfastly in his newfound faith.

It was four decades later that I met Robert. Sarah was celebrating her eighty-first birthday, and her children and grandchildren had gathered around her to reminisce. The air was full of laughter as one by one they shared their stories.

When Robert finally stood to speak, he did his best to fight back tears. He didn't mention what had happened one summer so many years earlier; there were many in the room who knew nothing about that. To look at him now, you might have guessed—rightly—that Robert had been a Sunday school teacher for years, had raised children of his own, and loved his mother deeply.

You might have also noticed, from their shared glances, a special understanding between them, like that of two people who had returned from a long and difficult journey with a story known only to each other. Robert wrapped up his thoughts with his own rendition of a well-known poem, changing only two words in the last line.

> You may have tangible wealth untold;
> Caskets of jewels and coffers of gold.
> Richer than I you can never be—
> I had a mother who *prayed for* me.[13]

When we give our children the gift of our prayers, we give them a future where hope awaits them in unexpected places. We discover that even miracles are possible through the strength of a Savior whose "love is better than life" (Psalm 63:3). And He does "all things well" (Mark 7:37[2]).

ACKNOWLEDGMENTS

So many have poured prayer into this book that I cannot thank them all. But may I try?

The people of Peace Church in Durham have faithfully encouraged and walked with me step-by-step, up to the throne of grace and back again. I would rather sit beside you at Jesus's feet than anywhere else.

Faithful readers and friends—many of whom I haven't met (*yet*)—have loved my family and me with your prayers as if we were your own. I look forward to one day looking back with you at all that your prayers have won. And it is already much.

I'm grateful for the hands and hearts that have influenced this book over the years. Joel Armstrong, Dawn Anderson, Miranda Gardner, and Paul Muckley, how blessed I am to have such skillful (and patient and faithful) editors who run to the Father as you work. Chriscynethia Floyd, how grateful I am to have a publisher with a renewed vision for this work! God's creativity, love, and attention to detail move through all of you (and the larger team) at Our Daily Bread Publishing to reach others in immeasurable, eternal ways. Working with you is the privilege of a lifetime.

So many friends along the way . . . John Holecek, Daniel and Jordan Henderson, Joel Collier, Don Westbrook, Dub

Karriker, Garth Rosell, Bob Mayer, Ken Davis, Lynn Wiemann, Dennis Carey, Mary and Dan Eakright, David Beaty, David McClean, Gary McGhee, Bob and Pam Dodson, Mark and Skip Honeck, Allen and Cathleen Huff . . . Heaven has heard you more than once on my behalf!

Stef and Geoff, this book couldn't have been written without you. I'm so thankful to be your dad. Thank you for your courage in letting me share some of your stories. Austin and Leilani, the prayers in this book are for you also (and all who may follow!).

Cari, you have once again lived up to the meaning of your name (Cari is short for Caridad, meaning "Charity"). Your faithfulness in daily life together and in consistent prayer for your husband and children is a priceless gift from God.

It is for the Gift above all gifts, the One who is at the right hand of the Father "pleading for us" (Romans 8:34[1]), that this book has been written. I would be lost without His love. Beautiful Savior, I pray these prayers may be used to bring you the "praise and honor and glory" (Revelation 5:13) that you deserve forever!

NOTES

5. All Scripture references throughout marked with a number 5—1 John 3:1[5]—are taken from the New American Standard Bible®, copyright © 1960, 1971, 1977, 1995, 2020 by The Lockman Foundation. Used by permission. All rights reserved. lockman.org.

6. Robert Browning, "Andrea del Sarto," Poetry Foundation, accessed April 17, 2024, https://www.poetryfoundation .org/poems/43745/andrea-del-sarto. Originally published 1855.

7. For more on this concept as it relates to prayer, please see Daniel Henderson, *Fresh Encounters: Experiencing Transformation through United Worship-Based Prayer* (Colorado Springs: NavPress, 2004), 90–91.

8. Bob Nightengale, "Pastor Strawberry Says True Calling Ahead, Not Baseball," *USA Today*, July 12, 2013, http:// www.usatoday.com/story/sports/mlb/2013/07/11/darryl -strawberry-tracy-strawberry-ministries-new-york-mets -drugs/2509921/.

9. Ruth Bell Graham, *Prodigals and Those Who Love Them* (Grand Rapids, MI: Baker, 1999), 75.

10. Arthur Bennett, ed., *The Valley of Vision: A Collection of Puritan Prayers and Devotions* (Edinburgh, Scotland: The Banner of Truth Trust, 1975), xxiv.

11. J. C. Ryle, "Are You Fighting?" SermonIndex.net, accessed April 17, 2024, www.sermonindex.net/modules/articles /index.php?view=article&aid=2331.

12. C. S. Lewis, *The Last Battle* (New York: Collier Books, 1980), 184.

13. Strickland Gillilan, "The Reading Mother," Public Domain Poetry, accessed April 17, 2024, https://poetscollective.org /publicdomain/the-reading-mother/.

INDEX

ABOUT THE AUTHOR

James Banks's books have encouraged people all over the world to pray. Among his many books are *Peace through Prayer*, *Prayers for Prodigals*, *Praying the Prayers of the Bible*, and *Hope Lies Ahead*, coauthored with his son, Geoffrey. James and his wife, Cari, make their home in Durham, North Carolina, where he is the founding pastor of Peace Church. James is a much-loved writer for the *Our Daily Bread* monthly devotional, and is featured on the weekly *Encouraging Prayer* radio broadcast and podcast. He is a popular speaker at conferences, retreats, and special events. To learn more, visit JamesBanks.org.